FIRST EDITION

Published by
Donn Larson

Copyright © 2018

Design by Julie Martin. Cover image by Jacob Boomsma.

International Standard Book Number
ISBN 978-0-692-17177-6 US $20.00

Printed in the United States of America
by JS Print Group, Inc., Duluth, MN

THE WILL

AND

THE WAY

VOLUME II

LEADERSHIP STORIES SHAPING DULUTH'S BRIGHT FUTURE

Assembled with care and affection
for their community

by

Donn Larson

Jessica Tillman, Editor

Julie Martin, Designer

and

Volunteer Community Writers

ACKNOWLEDGMENTS

The ability to compile and publish *The Will and the Way, Volume II* depended upon generous supporters, to whom we owe thanks.

Launching this project has been funded in large part by the Community Leaders Fund of the Duluth Superior Area Community Foundation.

Zeitgeist Center for Arts & Community has supported this project as the non-profit fiscal agent. All profits from the sale of this book will support Zeitgeist's ongoing community leadership initiatives.

Contribution from The Ben and Jeanne Overman Charitable Trust, and Andy Goldfine, Ken Goldfine, and Ellen Troeltzsch also helped launch the project.

Konnie LeMay, Cindy Marshall Hayden, and Paul Hayden offered advice and expertise in the process of preparing the book for press.

David Ouse contributed his talents as a writer, historian and researcher, finding aptly inspiring and relevant quotes to begin each of the seven sections in this book.

Felicia Schneiderhan served as a writer-editor, helping some of our authors get their stories on the page. Felicia's brilliant writing skills have been key to completing this compilation.

Thank you to Jacob Boomsma, the talented photographer who captured the cover image.

Mayor Emily Larson wrote the Epilogue, and thanks to her, this book ends on point. Her strong and encouraging voice makes the perfect sign-off.

Thanks to our printer, Tobbi Stager and JS Print Group, for their fine work and advice.

Thanks to Barb Darland, Lisa Bodine, Pascha Apter and the rest of the brilliant team at Giant Voices, who led our marketing efforts to make sure this book ended up in your hands.

And to you, dear reader, thank you for picking up this book, for caring about and taking an interest in our community, and for your role in Duluth's success.

Thank you to our families for supporting our long hours of work on this book.

It strains our vocabulary to express our gratitude to our friend Don Ness, who made sure we emphasized leaders from his generation. Don has been our utility outfielder, helping with marketing, distribution, promotion, and various tasks less fun than writing, editing, and recruiting others to lend their talent. When you see him, tell him you like *Volume II*.

Thank you to every citizen who played a role in projects revisited in these stories. These steady and often painstaking efforts have changed our community.

And of course, this compilation of stories is possible because authors and their collaborators donated their time and talent to present these words and images, which now comprise *The Will and the Way, Volume II*, to inspire future leaders and preserve the achievements of their generation.

With gratitude,

Donn Larson
Jessica Tillman, Editor
Julie Martin, Designer

THE WILL *and the* WAY, VOLUME II

TABLE OF SUBJECTS

FOREWORD

by Don Ness

American history is typically told through the stories of presidents, wars, macroeconomics and demographic trends — clearly important — but they don't tell the whole story. The truth of America's strength is not found in Washington D.C.; it's found in places like Duluth.

Duluth's remarkable recovery and revitalization over the past 30 years is worthy of study and celebration. By understanding our motivations, struggles and accomplishments in this rugged, industrial city, we learn of the everyday effort that refreshes our country, neighborhood by neighborhood, business by business, family by family.

Understanding a city through the lens of its most ambitious projects is a study of psychology, economics, human nature, leadership and priorities. The voices of optimistic leaders are consistently countered by the sideline critics' ready scorn. The best-laid plans are often frustrated by a steady stream of challenges. The possibility of failure hangs overhead like the sword of Damocles.

Every city is a compounding of generations of leaders, who, in their time engaged in turmoil that characterizes local leadership. Their decisions, initiatives, skirmishes, successes and failures all contributed to the city we see around us. Senators can pass laws in the halls of Congress, but the work of strengthening our country comes to life in places like Duluth.

When the first volume of *The Will and the Way* was published in 2004, I was just leaving my 20s and still on the Duluth City Council.

I found the book to be such a gift to the community. I read in awe and felt a deep appreciation for how those leaders dedicated themselves to overcome doubts and challenges, creating positive change that clearly helped shape Duluth.

I was inspired by the stories of community leaders who, by sheer will, force of personality, and love for their city, set forth an ambitious vision and committed themselves to seeing that vision come to life.

What struck me then is how little I knew about the background stories of how these projects came to be. Growing up here, I simply took for granted that Duluth had so much to offer, despite being a relatively small city. Only after I read *The Will and the Way* did I come to appreciate there was nothing inevitable about these achievements. These successes happened because community leaders had the will and found the way.

Over the past 20 years, Duluth's history has taken a sharp turn towards a more ambitious, confident, and optimistic posture. Duluth's reputation in the region has steadily improved as we have demonstrated civic courage to address our most significant problems and have found opportunities to lift up and celebrate the entrepreneurial success of business and community leaders.

This new book is a modest but devoted effort to collect, cultivate and promote community-based success stories of the current generation of leaders committed to Duluth's progress.

For every story told here, there are numerous different perspectives, other projects and efforts well worth telling and preserving. This book should be twice as long; there are so many more projects to celebrate. No collection of this scale could possibly be a complete one. The stories that make this city are countless and intertwined. And these stories — told in this book, in other texts and mediums, and those unrecorded or in the making — help compose the Duluth we experience today, personally and collectively.

In these pages, you will find stories of courage, skill and hard work. You'll find stories of coalitions of Duluthians often setting aside their differences in order to accomplish together more than they could alone. You'll find stories of visionaries that chose to exercise their talents in Duluth rather than on the larger stage of a big metro area.

You'll find stories of sacrifice, uncertainty and struggle. But, most of all, you'll find stories that reflect community pride and love for this beautiful little city, built on the side of a rocky hill, overlooking the world's greatest lake.

This book is a true community collaboration. At the center stands a dedicated team who pulled it all together.

Julie Martin, who designed the first volume, rebuilt the layout to fit a different organizational approach this time around, and in doing so, created cohesiveness and continuity across both volumes. Her years of design experience and her commitment to seeing the vision through drove this project forward. What you see in these pages is Julie's artistry and her high level of care about reflecting the importance of these stories in the design.

Jessica Tillman edited *Volume II*, cover to cover. She managed the project from the start, coordinated the collection of stories and images, and worked individually with each author to develop their respective chapters. Her commitment to honoring each writer's style and story gives the book a unique rhythm. Jessica has been the driving force behind this project — her encouragement, attention to detail, and determination made this project possible.

More than 40 community writers volunteered their time and talent to this book. One of my favorite characteristics of the book is its varying style — every chapter reads differently and reflects the array of perspectives necessary to make these projects happen. The commitment of these volunteer writers is the backbone of *The Will and the Way, Volume II*. Each writer honored the significance of their subject, completed the arduous work of recording their story, and gifted their time and energy to the project.

Donn Larson is the visionary behind both volumes of *The Will and the Way*. He partnered with the late Monnie Goldfine to publish the original and honored that partnership again in publishing the second volume.

Donn is a lifelong Duluthian, and his knowledge of this place is deep, reaching, and always recalled with care and respect for the people who make up our community. He and his wife Donna turned away opportunities to live and work in other parts of the world, choosing instead to root themselves in Duluth. They raised a family on Park Point, and are now enjoying a long retirement in this community.

When the prospect of a second volume surfaced, Donn committed whole-heartedly, and he and Donna graciously provided the book team a quiet, comfortable place to convene and work. Donn's voice and wisdom are woven through every element of this book. Both volumes exhibit Donn's talents in writing, storytelling, and drawing together community members to collaborate. His perspective is rare and invaluable, not just to a historical record like this book, but to the prosperity of our community. Like the original, we hope this second volume will become treasured and iconic in our region.

In celebrating Duluth's recent successes in *Volume II*, we hope to encourage and inspire the next generation to lead the city to ever-greater achievement in problem solving, strengthening our local economy, and contributing to this unique and special place.

The dramatic story of America will continue to evolve, but in Duluth, we will contribute to the broader narrative a compelling example of the strength of community. The stories for *Volume III* are beginning to take shape. We have an energetic new mayor, fresh goals, and exciting opportunities. And from within this virtuous cycle of supportive and aspirational leadership, there's no doubt in my mind that Duluth's best days are yet to come. ∎

Don Ness is executive director of the Ordean Foundation, an organization focused on addressing poverty issues in Duluth. Previously, Don has served for 16 years in elected leadership, culminating with a 91 percent job approval rating in his role as mayor of Duluth. Don's core values include a deep dedication to his family, and an ongoing spirit of service to his community. He and his wife Laura continue to live in Duluth with their three children: Ella, James, and Owen.

PREFACE

TO ACKNOWLEDGE LEADERS WE HAVE LOST

by Donn Larson

The original volume of *The Will and the Way* was published in 2004, so nearly 15 years have intervened. We're impressed Duluth's cultural and business momentum warrants a second book in such a short time. Leadership is increasingly energized in our community and we toast the host of writers and subjects that justify this new book. At the same time we want to acknowledge those leaders who gave so much substance in recent years whose lives have ended since its publication.

For starters I cite my 2004 co-publisher, **Monnie Goldfine**, who devoted himself to a succession of achievements like the original Arena-Auditorium and its expansions, Spirit Mountain, our Great Lakes Aquarium, and who advocated taxing visitors to support further promotion of a flourishing tourist industry. His brother **Irwin Goldfine**, was just as strongly motivated to contribute, especially in his service to UMD and 12 years as a University of Minnesota regent.

Another consummate organizer was **Charlie Bell**, who fell short in a couple of mayoral bids, but kept a family tradition for years as the informal mayor of western Duluth. Among many pursuits he was a partner in CNN Properties, chair of the Duluth Area Chamber of Commerce, president of Ordean Foundation and Boys and Girls Club.

In 2016 we lost **Bob Mars** who managed his business with one hand while the other hand was sculpting a stronger community.

All of us who were on Bob's mailing list know the scores of causes and candidates he supported. Bob was a charter member of Men as Peacemakers and served many years on the Duluth School Board.

Jeno Paulucci wrote Chapter 1 of our 2004 book. His candor stirred the reader to keep turning pages to find out what else had been happening. Jeno and Lois died just days apart in 2011, both leaving a legacy of lasting contributions to our city. The 1965 conversion of a scrapyard to our arena site had many advocates, but Jeno was clearly the spark from which that project and a continuing flow of waterfront improvements were kindled. We thank **Lois Paulucci** for one of the harbor's more recent advancements, Bayfront Festival Park.

We lost **Rob Link** when he was just 66. Rob came here in 1985 to manage the Jamar Co., then eased into the development business with partner Lee Anderson. His gift was the ability to recognize opportunity others could not see. His long list of commercial properties included the successful Tech Village, Wieland Block, Phoenix Building, Duluth Athletic Club and Lakewalk Surgery Center.

Shirley Bergum died in 2017. She was the engine that powered the Junior League's campaign to save the Union Depot from succumbing to decay, and led the early effort to restore and promote Glensheen. Both foresights have proved sound and prized today.

2017 also claimed two stalwarts of the Duluth Playhouse and countless other civic and cultural pursuits, **Selma** and **Dr. Bob Goldish**, who like the Pauluccis, died just four days apart.

Duluth's Loaves and Fishes community has many facets, especially its dedication to providing hospitality to people experiencing homelessness. Its co-founder, **Steve O'Neil**, St. Louis County commissioner, is memorialized in the Steve O'Neil Apartment complex, a six-unit emergency family shelter and 44 units of permanent supportive housing for homeless families with children.

Joan Henrik was only occasionally in the limelight, due mainly to her quiet modesty, but as a member of the Duluth Public Arts Commission she showed her passion for public art and its ability to build a better community. She compiled a comprehensive inventory of Duluth's public art and made her own mark in functional art at the DECC, where she earned one of her 125 design awards.

John Steffl lost a long battle with cancer in June, 2018. John's dedication to the visual arts at the Duluth Art Institute, Tweed Museum, College of St. Scholastica, as well as business venues like Lizzards Gallery and North Shore Bank, made him a champion of the art scene whose influence will long be prominent.

Meg Bye had a keen eye for accomplishment in local government and served as Duluth's first Human Rights Officer. Another prominent example of women stepping into the ranks of leadership was **Isobel Rapaich**, who represented the fifth District on Duluth's first council with women in the majority. Among her active interests was our Sister Cities program.

Jackie Morris, Jim Oberstar's district manager, died in 2016, two years after the death of her congressman. Diligently working behind the scenes, she served our Eighth District representative during the entire 36 years he was in office.

Duluth's distinguished paleopathologist, **Dr. Arthur Aufderheide**, died in 2013. His wife and partner, **Mary Aufderheide**, who assisted in his research, died in 2017. Both were dedicated Duluthians as well as internationally acclaimed for their pioneering study of mummies.

Two local military heroes left our ranks since *Volume 1* was published. During World War II, **Joe Gomer** was a member of the Tuskegee Airmen, our country's first black fighter squadron, a welcome indication of integration in the military that eventually happened in 1948. He flew 68 combat missions, survived a crash landing, and received the Congressional Gold Medal in 2007 from President Bush. Duluth's Congressional Medal of Honor recipient, **Mike Colalillo**, died in 2011 at 86. In April '45, near Untrgriesheim, Germany, he led his comrades toward enemy fire, and routed their emplacement, silencing all resistance in the area and helped a wounded soldier make his way back to the American line. The Medal of Honor is the U.S. military's highest decoration.

Al Amatuzio, a veteran of the U.S. Navy, Air Force and Air National Guard, dedicated himself to proving synthetic oil would better automobile engine lubrication as it had benefitted military aircraft. He developed and introduced AMSOIL, copied today by every oil company in America. The success of his product resulted in a six-million-dollar sponsorship of Duluth's AMSOIL Arena.

Al France, who wrote about the Taconite Constitutional Amendment in *Volume I*, died in 2015. Al played a key role in the development of Minnesota's iron mining industry as president of its trade association, served four terms in the legislature, and was recognized for his civic leadership when elected to the Duluth Hall of Fame.

Those who knew Eighth District Court of Appeals Judge **Gerald Heaney** will agree that the sobriquet *éminence grise* suits him well. Duluth lost his quiet and effective leadership in 2010. Judge Heaney accomplished a distinguished career in the military, engaged in civic activity and served 40 years in the judiciary.

Ellen Pence, who created the Duluth Model of intervention in domestic violence cases, a widely copied collaborative approach, had her career cut short in 2012 by breast cancer at age 63.

Alzheimer's took **Lauren Larsen** from Duluth's leadership ranks. Lauren co-founded the LHB engineering firm that has grown from two to 260 professional engineers and architects. His first client was the Duluth Arena in 1963.

We remember **Nick Smith** for his tenacity in founding Lake Superior Center which became our Great Lakes Aquarium, and his enterprising venture capital initiative, Northeast Ventures and its sibling Northeast Entrepreneur Fund.

Several of the Duluthians mentioned above wrote chapters in *Volume I*, but there were other authors who are no longer with us. **Walker Jamar, Jr.**, a two-term councilor covered the Lyric Block redevelopment and the Gateway Urban Renewal Project, which he was instrumental in organizing as a facelift for our downtown's western portal. **Bob Prescott**, active in civic ventures throughout his career, wrote about the Radisson Hotel; Bob also served on the city council, and was the Arena Auditorium Administrative Board's first president. **Bob Eaton**, another councilor of the '60s, described the gestation and growing pains of Miller Hill Mall. **Bruce Buchanan** told us about the YMCA from his perspective as the leading fundraiser for its 1963 construction and $1.5-million expansion in 1980.

Harry Munger left us just a few months before this book was printed. Harry loved political action and brought his lawyerly persuasiveness to his party, his community and many conservation causes.

Family and friends also celebrated the life of **Linnea Stephan** in January 2018, integral in building the Center for Changing Lives, intent on ending youth homelessness; and of **Peggy Atmore Mason** in August 2018, founder of the Atmore Memorial Ski Race in the 1970s.

Agreeing to write about leaders we've lost since 2004 includes accepting the risk of missing some, maybe several. I accept this consequence and apologize to friends and families of those omitted.

To quote (with some paraphrasing) a few lines from a David Brooks October 2016 *New York Times* column: "A healthy community isn't just an atomized mass of individual economic and legal units. A community is a web of giving and getting. You give to your job and your employer gives to you. You give to your neighborhood, and your neighborhood gives to you. You give to your government and your government gives to you... The citizen enjoys a sweet reverence for all the gifts that have been handed down over time, and a generous piety about community that is the opposite of arrogance."

How fortunate it is that a generous piety pervades our city, invigorating both the will and the way to fix, foster and secure our "web of giving and getting." ∎

Donn Larson co-published the original 2004-05 edition of The Will and the Way *with his friend, the late Monnie Goldfine. He has long been active in civic and cultural affairs, starting as a city councilor in 1959. He has since contributed his time and energy in many places, among them the Arena/ Auditorium Board, Duluth–Superior Area Community Foundation, City Planning Commission, and the Great Lakes Aquarium.*

INDUSTRIES

"A city is not gauged by its length and width,
but by the broadness of its vision and the height of its dreams."

—Herb Caen, San Francisco Examiner columnist

CHAPTER

1

AAR's Arrival in Duluth

AVIATION THRIVES IN THE TWIN PORTS

by Brian Hanson

This story began in 2005 when Northwest Airlines (NWA) made the decision to close its 400-person aircraft maintenance facility at the Duluth International Airport. The facility had been built for NWA by the State of Minnesota in 1999 to incent the airline to keep its hub and headquarters at Minneapolis-Saint Paul International Airport — part of a multi-community package designed to boost both the company and a struggling northeast Minnesota economy. But labor challenges and industry trends to cut costs and outsource maintenance services prompted NWA to negotiate an early out of agreements with the State and close the facility.

State and City officials recognized the value in local control and ownership of the 189,000-square-foot maintenance facility, and upon its closure, deeded it to the Duluth Economic Development Authority (DEDA). DEDA launched a nationwide search for a new tenant, while also considering a solid and growing airport tenant close to home, Cirrus Design. Cirrus entered into a 25-year lease with DEDA for the facility starting in 2008, intending to use it as the design center for the Cirrus Vision Jet. When the recession hit in 2009, luxury products like small aircraft were particularly vulnerable, and hard times set in at Cirrus. Faced with several rounds of layoffs, lost sales orders, ownership struggles, and severe financial difficulty, Cirrus couldn't meet lease obligations and sought forgiveness and release from the contract.

In the midst of negotiation with Cirrus, DEDA underwent significant organizational changes, moving from a city-council-led authority to a public-private partnership model. The City's Chief Administrative Officer David Montgomery shepherded DEDA through negotiation and transition in the absence of an executive director. I joined the newly configured DEDA as a citizen member, and thus, my journey with the aircraft maintenance facility project began.

Under Montgomery and Mayor Don Ness's leadership, DEDA obliged Cirrus' request, securing commitment from the company to new investment and returned jobs once growth resumed.

The need for official DEDA leadership impended. Montgomery's interim directorship served the organization well, and it was time to enter the next stage. My friends and economic development colleagues urged me to consider joining the City's business development team, which would allow me to transition from a DEDA commissioner to its executive director. My love for this city, and my commitment to our potential, led me to heed the call in January 2010.

The City's Land and Business Development departments had merged, leveraging staff's property management expertise for better services toward growing local business. Our newly formed team, and the underutilized aircraft maintenance facility, melded into an incredible opportunity.

A maintenance facility task force convened to research and identify best potential tenants. I co-led the task force alongside Rob West,

CEO of APEX, a trusted private sector business development partner with a special knack for industry research and targeted recruitment. Other key task force members included Brian Ryks of the Duluth Airport Authority, Don Monaco of DEDA and Monaco Air, Chris Maddy of the Northspan Group, Mike Lundstrom of the Hermantown Area Chamber of Commerce, and Mark McShane of the City's Business Development Department. Stan Melling assisted the task force as a contract consultant — Melling had helped design and operate the facility for NWA. His willingness to help, his knowledge of the aircraft maintenance industry, and his deep industry relationships were key to the project's eventual success.

On the facility side, DEDA contracted with another former NWA employee, Rand Lally, to ensure adequate maintenance, security, and upkeep. We relied on Lally to answer detailed questions about building systems and features during facility tours. His knowledge impressed our visitors, and more importantly, kept everyone safe while touring the site.

The task force assessed the market, developed a potential tenant list, designed marketing materials, and began making contacts. In April 2011, opportunity arose; the aviation industry's maintenance, repair and overhaul (MRO) trade event, called "MRO Americas," hosted professionals from many of our target aviation companies, all in one place.

West, Melling, and I arrived at "MRO Americas" prepared to find a tenant. We had previously briefed DEDA commissioners on our goals for the project: create jobs, eliminate DEDA's facility-carrying costs and maintenance responsibilities (about $15,000 a month), and secure a long-term lease agreement with a leading MRO company. Lofty goals, especially considering the event drew in people selling competing facilities all around the country, and the world. We crafted an attractive deal featuring a competitive facility lease rate and promised assistance with employee attraction, financing, and training. We met 17 of our 25 target tenants, ending our visit with a stop at our top candidate's booth, a Chicago-based company called AAR.

AAR's salesman listened to our pitch. We didn't expect what happened next. The salesman asked us to stop back later to meet the

Front: Danny Martinez and Don Ness shake hands following AAR's commitment to Duluth. (2012) *Back:* Brian Hanson, Linda Krug, the late Steve O'Neil, Emily Larson, David Ross, Rob West, Chris Dahlberg, John Heino, Brian Ryks.

president of the company! Of course, we did; and in that meeting, AAR's president, Tim Romenesko, said he'd learned of our facility years ago when the late Representative Jim Oberstar pitched it to him. Romenesko said that while AAR had no immediate expansion plans, he would keep it in mind and stay in touch.

Less than two weeks later, Romenesko proved to be a man of his word. I received a call from AAR's Danny Martinez, who was tasked with visiting our facility. When he asked about a date that would work for us, I responded, "Today would be great!"

Martinez arrived in Duluth the following week. Lally provided an insider's tour of the facility. We talked aircraft maintenance, and thanks to Lake Superior's relentless power, we also talked fishing. Martinez left us impressed with AAR. Several more visits followed; we met other AAR leaders and technicians from their sites at Indianapolis, Oklahoma City, and Miami. They carefully considered the facility, the community, and the airport. A question arose: can both AAR and Cirrus be successful here? To that, Cirrus executives welcomed AAR, courageously accepting risks of competition in support of building a thriving airport community.

Although the facility was a shoo-in, Duluth would be a small city for AAR. How could they ever recruit the needed workforce and skills in a comparatively small metro area? Our team offered to prove our workforce by holding a job fair. AAR agreed to put their name on the event, and the "AAR Career & Networking Fair" came to life with the help of DECC Executive Director Dan Russell and his exceptional crew. A similar event had recently been held in Salinas, Kansas with limited success — fewer than 100 people attended, only some of whom were qualified. Duluth's two-day event attracted more than 300 people, including many airframe and powerplant (A&P) mechanics.

Greg Dellinger, chief recruiter for AAR, seemed pleased by the event. However, when I asked him about his schedule for the next day, he said he was taking off in the morning. I was crestfallen. How could he leave? Didn't we meet his expectations?

"I saw everything I needed today to know that AAR can be a success in Duluth," he said.

The following months were a whirlwind of details and visits to and from AAR headquarters in Wood Dale, IL. DEDA commissioners Don Monaco and Nancy Norr joined the visits to Wood Dale, along with Commissioner Mark Phillips of the Minnesota Department of Employment and Economic Development (DEED). Rob West of APEX provided helpful mentoring on positioning Duluth for the next AAR expansion, and served as the quintessential host to AAR staff.

By the spring of 2012, AAR was committed to Duluth. Now all they needed was a customer. AAR was working closely with Air Canada,

The important work of aircraft maintenance keeps the skies safe for all of us.

and that contract would need a home. Air Canada was convinced that they needed to be in an existing facility with a revenue-producing route, like Indianapolis or Miami. AAR was convinced Air Canada could fill the Duluth facility. Now, our job was to help AAR prove it.

Air Canada visited AAR's sites in Miami, Indianapolis, and Duluth. Several Duluth dignitaries met the AAR and Air Canada group, including Mayor Ness, Al Hodnik of ALLETE, Peter Hedstrom of US Bank, David Ross of the Duluth Area Chamber of Commerce, and members of the aforementioned task force. Lally once again ably led a detailed facility tour, establishing instant credibility with the Air Canada executives. We showed the community's support, made the facility shine, and proved our workforce was available and strong.

We soon learned the Duluth team impressed Air Canada, and serious negotiations had now begun. Our challenge was to sharpen the pencil on every financial aspect of the project. AAR needed the lowest facility cost possible to close the

"I saw everything I needed today to know that AAR can be a success in Duluth," he said.

deal. With help from the State of Minnesota, we delivered just that.

We thought the deal was in hand; then the State of Georgia offered a huge incentive to an MRO competing for Air Canada's business, reducing its cost by millions. Could we counter? Commissioner Phillips found resources to partially offset the Georgia incentive, and Governor Dayton approved. It wasn't the same huge amount, but together with the tremendous effort our community had made, it was enough to win the contract.

Today, AAR employs almost 400 people under the leadership of Mark Ketterer, primarily serving United Airlines. They are the industry leader in maintenance and a solid bedrock of the aviation cluster in this region. ∎

Brian Hanson became APEX's president and CEO in June 2012, bringing over 15 years of business and community development experience. His work has contributed to several significant regional business expansion, retention and attraction projects in industries including mining, engineering, manufacturing, heavy aircraft maintenance, aviation, and data centers. Brian, his wife Brenda, and children Alex and Sammy, enjoy live music, sports (GO DOGS!), cooking, gardening, and the great outdoors.

AUTHOR ACKNOWLEDGMENTS

DEDA Commissioners

Don Monaco, Chair
Nancy Norr, Vice Chair
John Heino
Christine Townsend
Jay Fosle
Dan Hartman
Emily Larson

City Staff & Attorneys

Heidi Timm-Bijold
Chris Eng
Bob Asleson
Joan Christensen

DEED Staff

Kevin McKinnon
Paul Moe
Heather Rand

St. Louis County

Kevin Gray
Mark Rubin
Barb Hayden

CHAPTER

2

Historic Arts & Theatre District

OLD DOWNTOWN CELEBRATES ARTS
AND ENTREPRENEURS

by Kristi Stokes

Downtown Duluth has gone through significant challenges over the course of the last couple decades. The challenges, however, have united our community behind a vision for a stronger, more vibrant downtown.

In my first month on the job at the Greater Downtown Council (GDC), property owner Lance Reasor delivered a heartfelt request: please pay attention to the Old Downtown. Lance's request was genuine, simple, and valid. And from the GDC's office, at that time in the Old Downtown, I saw a place with boundless potential.

In 2000, what was then called the Old Downtown was far from a shining star. Alternating old, desolate buildings and well-kept, bustling buildings created a mismatched streetscape. A&L Development had recently worked with the City of Duluth to develop the new Technology Village at the corner of Lake Avenue and Superior Street. Other than

Pakou Ly

Looking westward down the Superior Street corridor from Third Avenue East.

the Technology Village, most major investment and redevelopment in the downtown area was focused west of Lake Avenue.

The GDC accepted the challenge to show the community what promise hid in the quiet, storied eastern downtown. We started small with something we were good at — a special event. The GDC created a classic car show just for the Old Downtown, and Rob Link of A&L, developer of the aforementioned Tech Village, was one of the first to jump on board as a sponsor. Two years in, the car show had grown, stretching from 3rd Avenue East westward, across Lake Avenue, and all the way to 5th Avenue West. It remains an annual event today, attracting more than 500 classic cars each summer and thousands of car-show enthusiasts.

The GDC also pursued the creation of a special service district throughout downtown, in which property owners agreed to pay a fee for GDC services and programs. By pooling their resources,

Terri Alexander

Looking eastward down the Superior Street corridor from Lake Avenue.

with a designated match from the City of Duluth, the GDC began providing safety and hospitality services through its uniformed Clean & Safe Team. In addition, we improved public spaces and increased marketing efforts. Newfound understanding and recognition of the GDC as the downtown's management organization fostered a growing sense of downtown stewardship.

Property owners pursued substantial changes of their own. The medical district was poised to grow as both Essentia Health and St. Luke's Hospital expanded, bringing them closer to Old Downtown's Superior Street. Sherman Associates partnered with Essentia and the city to acquire the property now home to the Sheraton Hotel and condos, blending housing and hospitality. The Zeppa Foundation purchased the Red Lion Bar and neighboring property to develop an independent theater and café, Zeitgeist Arts, through which it continues its arts cultivation and community-building. Many other

Last Place on Earth

DULUTH'S THREE-YEAR BATTLE TO RESCUE
OLD DOWNTOWN FROM THE RISE OF
A PUBLIC HEALTH PANDEMIC

by Nathan LaCoursiere

For many years, Old Downtown was home to the well-known head shop called "Last Place on Earth" or "LPOE." Owned by Jim Carlson, the business was located at 120 E. Superior Street – right in the heart of Duluth's historic downtown district.

During the summer of 2010, LPOE began selling addictive and harmful synthetic drug products commonly known and marketed as "legal alternatives," "incense," "bath salts," "watch cleaner," "pipe cleaner," and so on. The products were labeled "not fit for human consumption," although everyone knew that

Kip Praslowicz

developments followed, including the renovation of the old City Hall by the owners of the Brewhouse; full restoration of the Fannie Rose building; significant reinvestments at ShelDon Printing and Fond-du-Luth Casino; Black Woods restaurant expanded its services to downtown with its addition of Black Water martini bar and event programming and catering at Greysolon Ballroom; and Duluth Trading Company returned to its roots to open a storefront.

By 2011, a new era for an old downtown had gained significant momentum. But a simmering challenge in the middle of it all pushed Duluth into the national spotlight, and not in a positive way.

Lines of people, often 30 to 40 deep, formed daily outside the doors of 120 East Superior Street – the Last Place on Earth headshop, which prided itself on the sale of synthetic drugs. The growing crowd of people outside the store regularly caused police

Last Place on Earth

customers were purchasing the products to get high. At the time, the nation was slowly waking to this new public health threat. Duluth had the misfortune of being on the front lines of this emerging drug trend and swiftly became ground zero in the national war on synthetic drugs. By 2011, LPOE was selling synthetics to upward of 1,000 customers a day – to the tune of $16,000 a day or $6 million in revenue a year.

Nuisance conditions flowing from the sale of synthetics at LPOE quickly overwhelmed Old Downtown. Customers clogged the sidewalk in both directions every day, blocking access to neighboring businesses. Police calls skyrocketed – the Duluth Police Department received 2,843 calls for service to the block over a 12-month period alone. Nearby building owners reported finding vomit, urine and human feces in their entryways. Pedestrians were solicited, panhandled, and verbally abused.

City, community and business leaders responded quickly, calling on Carlson to end LPOE's damaging trade. Carlson declined, adopting an aggressive and well-financed legal defense. It was clear that, in the absence of a creative, determined, and multi-faceted public-private approach, Carlson would never stop selling synthetics.

In early 2011, community leaders started building coalitions and strategies to tackle the problem on all fronts. Local law enforcement worked closely with public attorneys to gather evidence in support of public nuisance actions and criminal prosecutions. The city labored to craft ordinances broad enough to encompass

Continued on next page

Last Place on Earth

Continued from previous page

synthetic drugs.

Events moved quickly. The city commenced its first public nuisance action in early 2012, obtaining an order requiring LPOE to pay city police costs for nuisance enforcement. In December 2012, Carlson was indicted by the United States Attorney's Office on over 50 counts of violating federal controlled substance and FDA laws. Carlson defiantly continued selling, resulting in two additional city nuisance actions and a city licensing ordinance that ultimately forced closure of the business on July 19, 2013.

LPOE never reopened. In October 2013, a federal jury convicted Carlson on 51 of 55 counts of violating federal drug laws. Carlson was sentenced to 17 ½ years in prison. United States Marshals took possession of the business, removing the iconic signage from LPOE's façade and readying the building for sale. The building was subsequently sold to Titanium Partners, LLC, a local real estate development firm led

calls, disrupted passers-by and customers to neighboring businesses, increased panhandling, and brought about disturbing behavior. The scene drew attention and quickly became known as the black eye of downtown. Duluth was now at the forefront of a national conversation about synthetic drugs and the impact of their sale on a community.

In the one and only meeting I had with LPOE owner Jim Carlson, he said he wasn't doing anything wrong and didn't seem concerned about his shop's negative impact on neighboring businesses.

Mayor Don Ness, former Police Chief Gordon Ramsay and the Duluth Police Department, and the City Attorney's Office worked arduously to end the headshop's effects on our community. Distributors of synthetics continuously changed the make-up of their products, staying one step ahead of the law. Their strategy prompted our local legislative delegation to craft new state laws. Our businesses and property owners remained vocal and united through the entire ordeal.

In mid-2013, the City of Duluth gained a temporary restraining order to close the business after police made a controlled buy of synthetic drugs the store was not licensed to sell. It remained closed while legal issues proceeded through court. Then in October of that year, a federal jury convicted Jim Carlson of 51 counts related to selling synthetic drugs. He was eventually sentenced to 17 ½ years in federal prison, and U.S.

Marshals seized the building, ending the public nuisance. Justice was served.

The tide changed immediately. Neighboring businesses saw increases in walk-in traffic. A survey by the GDC indicated that 45 percent of respondents said the downtown was more inviting. Plus, 39 percent said it felt safer. We were turning the page to a new chapter in our Old Downtown.

The renewed sense of optimism and energy prompted an effort to rename Old Downtown. Rod Raymond, downtown business owner, led a grassroots effort with neighboring businesses to rebrand the area. Thanks to the wealth of historic buildings, and infusion of arts, culture and entertainment, the area became known as the Historic Arts & Theatre District, or HART District. As an invested property owner in the district and a neighbor to the former LPOE, ShelDon Printing volunteered their services to create a dynamic new logo for the district. And former City Councilor Sharla Gardner advocated for city support of the district's new name and signage for the HART District public parking ramp.

Eventually, the federal government sold the LPOE building to Brian Forcier of Titanium Partners. At first, I didn't know if I should thank him for his interest in purchasing the building, or talk him out of it due to its poor condition. I'm glad he trusted his foresight. Now, the stunning storefront houses Blacklist Artisan Ales. Solve Entertainment, a company which

Last Place on Earth

by Brian and Monique Forcier. The building was substantially renovated and repurposed for a variety of different businesses and office space, including Blacklist Artisan Ales, a taproom and brewery playing an important role in Duluth's craft-beer boom. The Historic Downtown District as a whole sprang back to life with the closure of LPOE, sparking new creative and artistic endeavors in Old Downtown, renamed Duluth's Historic Arts & Theatre (HART) District. The joint, collaborative public approach to addressing this problem set a national precedent, and cities around the country continued seeking Duluth's counsel in addressing the synthetic drug pandemic for several years following the closure of LPOE.

Recreational and illegal drug use and sales, and the subsequent nuisance issues and impact on public health and safety, tend to evolve in communities. Public-private partnerships must evolve, too, in order to maintain and improve

Continued on next page

Last Place on Earth

Continued from previous page

a community's safety and vitality. In Duluth, bringing down LPOE strengthened partnerships imperative to community progress. The assembly and ultimate success of those partnerships represents a widespread commitment to a healthy place — a commitment sure to sustain the ability to work together and prevail for the good of the community, even when faced with complex, evolving challenges. ∎

Nathan LaCoursiere joined the Duluth City Attorney's Office in 2012. He was recognized as one of Minnesota's Up & Coming Attorneys in 2014 for his role in prosecuting the city's public nuisance actions against the Last Place on Earth. He dedicates his free time to his wife, Nora Sandstad, sons, Henry and Charlie, Duluth's world-class mountain bike system, and Wednesday night sailboat racing on the Great Lake they call Gitche Gumee.

produces live action physical adventure games called escape rooms, offices on the second floor.

Restoration of the historic NorShor Theatre bolsters optimism in the future of the HART District. The City of Duluth rescued the 1910 landmark when its economic development authority, DEDA, purchased the property in 2010. And thanks to a partnership with developer Sherman Associates and the Duluth Playhouse, the State designated bonding dollars toward the project. This multi-million-dollar makeover was completed in December 2017 and the NorShor shines again as a cultural anchor in the district. This investment has spurred other new investment in the neighborhood and will remain an economic development driver.

Transformation of Duluth's Old Downtown into today's HART District began years ago, piece by piece, as a community who cared rallied for investment and change. Today we share belief in the HART District's potential and vibrant future. It sets the perfect stage for the arts, retail, business, and crafts that happen there. The momentum has perhaps just picked up to the point of no return. ∎

Kristi Stokes has been the president of the Greater Downtown Council since 2000. When she is not downtown, she can often be found enjoying summer boating on Lake Superior with her husband, David, and son, Tanner.

3

Zeitgeist Center
for Arts & Community

BUILDING COMMUNITY, CREATIVELY

by Tony Cuneo

I first met Alan Zeppa in November of 2007 at a party to celebrate the opening of the Teatro Zuccone. The Teatro was, at that time, an all-new performance theater in the newly minted Zeitgeist Arts Building — one of the many innovative projects the Zeppa Foundation was a part of.

The A.H. Zeppa Family Foundation was Alan Zeppa's organization. It was obviously an intriguing subject to much of the community, me included. From seemingly out of nowhere there was a new organization in town making major contributions to nonprofits and investing in ideas that would change the way Duluth looked and felt. This was a rare opportunity for a community, and I was happy to have a chance to meet the man responsible for making it happen.

Performance theater entrance to the Zeitgeist Arts Building.

We were introduced and began chatting about various current affairs, both locally and nationally, and about his vision for the new theater and for his organization. Before we got too far in our conversation the rest of the party got in the way. He invited me to swing by his office in the next week so we could keep chatting. He struck me as funny and modest, and I liked him immediately.

Alan moved to the Twin Ports around 1983 and first settled in Superior, WI. He left after a couple of years to return to Iowa State University where he obtained a PhD in family environment in 1989. He returned to the Twin Ports a few years later and taught throughout the area, including at UMD and UWS.

On his way to the Twin Ports he asked some folks about Duluth and was told he was on his way to the "armpit of Minnesota." Fortunately, that didn't stop him.

In 2005 Alan inherited a block of United Parcel Service stock

Fair Food Access Campaign community meeting at Harrison Community Center in Duluth's Lincoln Park neighborhood.

his father had accumulated many years earlier, which had grown, essentially untouched, since the time of his father's death in 1953. One portion of the inheritance was targeted for charitable donations of Alan's choice. Recognizing the impact it could have on Duluth and the surrounding community, Alan made the decision to turn the charitable portion of the inheritance into a local foundation based here in the Twin Ports.

Alan could have simply turned his charitable obligations toward a favorite national nonprofit or two — it certainly would have been simpler, administratively. Or he could have set up an organization where he grew up, and where he expected to someday retire, in northern California. But in conversations with his children, they acknowledged the uniqueness of Duluth and the surrounding community and recognized the impact they could have on the Twin Ports. They realized investments made here had the potential to

Top: Singer/Songwriter Rachael Kilgour performs for a full house in the Zeitgeist performance theater (Teatro Zuccone).

Bottom: Theater 1 of the Zeitgeist movie theaters (Zinema).

make a real difference. For Alan's daughters, Duluth was home. For Alan, Duluth was the community where he had chosen to raise his family. Duluth was the place to set up shop.

It was a momentous decision that's had a deep impact on the character of our community. And it's an example of Duluth becoming a community of choice.

The Twin Ports were once widely derided as a community whose future was far from bright. But Alan and his family's decision to invest here is testament to the belief of many in our area that we live in one of the most unique, beautiful communities in the world.

The grants made by the Zeppa Foundation helped transform a number of local nonprofits working to reduce poverty, protect the environment, and enhance the cultural and artistic opportunities we have here. And while foundations are known for making positive change through their grants, the Zeppa Foundation went a step further.

> His vision to house community development, environmental protection, and support of the arts and culture all within one organization was inspiring.

The endowment also played an enormous role in shaping our community, making investments in local and regional software companies, commercial real estate, apartment buildings and housing developments, retail locations, restaurants, and performance venues. This approach to managing the endowment brought its own array of challenges and risks, but the incredible impact it had on the community can't be denied. Local and regional companies grew, jobs were created, and ideas were built that would otherwise still just be ideas.

In late 2008 the first waves of the great recession were being felt, just

Joe Olivieri

Riders gather for the start of the Mayor's Bike Ride, part of May's "Bus, Bike, Walk" celebration. (2018)

as the final plans for the Zeitgeist Arts Building were coming together. The Zeitgeist Arts Building is one of the signature achievements of the Zeppa Foundation. Built in part as a downtown revitalization project, the Zeitgeist Arts Building brought a performance theater, an independent movie theater, and a new restaurant and art gallery to our community. It helped spur the Historic Arts and Theater district, and has had a major influence in helping to define our community as one that invests in creativity, celebrating culture, and sharing the diverse stories and ideas of our citizens.

And while there was great excitement about this wonderful new project, internally it was mixed with a growing sense that we'd need to begin to rethink how we ran our organization. The endowment, while an incredible tool for helping to spur change in our community, was also invested in a highly risky, speculative fashion. Combined with the expenses of developing the Zeitgeist Arts Building, the subsequent intense cash needs of a startup restaurant, independent movie theater, and black box performance theater strained the endowment, which simply wasn't structured to withstand the major economic downturn in 2008 and 2009. While we weren't fully conscious of it yet, this was the beginning of the evolution of the Zeppa Foundation to the Zeitgeist Center for Arts & Community.

Today Zeitgeist, as a nonprofit, is unique in many ways, but like all nonprofits, Zeitgeist works each year to raise enough money through donations, sponsorships, grants, and earned income to fulfill its mission. But back then, as knowledge of the impact the recession had on our endowment spread to more of us at the organization, it became increasingly clear we were going to have to chart a new path forward. Increasingly, a number of us within the organization were finding ourselves in new leadership positions, collectively tasked with steering the organization towards a sustainable future.

Over time, this became a project we invited the whole community to be a part of. Alan Zeppa had served as the sole trustee at Zeppa since he founded the organization in 2005. His vision to house community development, environmental protection, and support of the arts and culture all within one organization was inspiring. To keep that vision strong, we needed the wisdom, diverse skill sets, and networks of support that only a broad local board could provide. And we knew that if we were going to ask for the community's support, we needed strong local leadership our community could trust to manage that support. Luckily, Alan's strong vision and the organization he set up attracted incredible local talent to commit their time and energy to our ever-changing organization.

In late 2014 we worked with the *Duluth News Tribune* to begin to explain our transition to the rest of the community. We described both the challenges and excitement of transitioning from the Zeppa Foundation to the Zeitgeist Center for Arts & Community. We didn't know if local foundations, who had known us as a funding partner, or the people and businesses of Duluth, who had known us as the philanthropic outcome of Alan's inheritance and generosity, would be open to changing the way they thought of us. So one by one we tested it, writing some small grants locally, working with some of our closest business relationships to develop sponsorship opportunities, and even hosting a small fundraiser just after the newspaper article in 2014. At each step we won enough support to indicate there was opportunity to keep building, keep working, and continue to fight for this organization.

And here Zeitgeist is today, a part of a new story being told about Duluth. The investments the Zeppa trusts made across our city helped change the face of who we are. The work Zeitgeist continues has helped Duluth become a community of choice, a place people fight for the opportunity to live in.

As every community does, we get to write our own story and shape our own identity. Zeitgeist relishes the chance to help. In fact, we'd say that's exactly the role we were born to play.

It's right there in the name: Zeitgeist, the spirit of the times. Zeitgeist's role is to help shape the spirit and define the character of our community. It's not any one program, or even the Zeitgeist Arts Building and all of the programs it houses, that ultimately defines our organization. Just like it's not any one policy or one neighborhood that defines our community. It's the values we commit to that shape decision after decision, action after action, that define us.

At Zeitgeist we're practicing the art of growing a connected community empowered to be creative and thrive. We're working to build community, creatively. This is the spirit that defines us, and the spirit that we hope will come to define our community for generations to come. ∎

Tony Cuneo lives in Duluth with his wife Erin and his four kids, Esmae, Elsa, Teva and Tuuli. Tony is the executive director of the Zeitgeist Center for Arts & Community, an arts and community development organization practicing the art of building a connected, creative, thriving community. Tony's past work includes community and issue-based organizing, a term on the Duluth City Council, and terms with the Duluth Economic Development Authority and the Duluth Housing and Redevelopment Authority. He's a graduate of UMD.

Trudy Vrieze

CHAPTER

4

Craft Brewing

DULUTH BECOMES THE CRAFT BEER CAPITAL
OF MINNESOTA

by Dave Hoops

In 2013, Duluth proclaimed itself The Craft Beer Capital of Minnesota (CBC of MN)™. One reason, Mayor Ness pointed out, was to beat the mayors of St. Paul and Minneapolis to the punch — a very astute and apropos move by Don, since all three cities had breweries with interesting and quality offerings popping up on almost every corner. The growth continues today; as of this writing, there are over 130 breweries in Minnesota, and without a doubt, Duluth has been a major force in Minnesota's craft beer surge.

When I moved to Duluth from San Francisco in 1999, there were only four craft breweries in Minnesota. Two of those were in Duluth: Lake Superior Brewery and Fitger's Brewhouse. Fast forward to 2018, and there are currently 16 active breweries in the region with up to six more breweries in planning or set to open. What an amazing

L Mclean

The Kettle Room at Fitger's Complex displays a collection of the old brewery's memorabilia, including a copper kettle used during the brewing process. The original brewery closed its doors in 1972. Today, the restored building has a hotel, shops, and restaurants – including Fitger's Brewhouse.

success story for brewers in northern Minnesota.

Many people ask: How did this happen? Why has craft beer become such a go-to for consumers? There are many reasons. The number one: people are committed to supporting local business and locally made goods. Small, craft breweries are as local as it gets. As the small brewery movement became the norm nationwide, the Twin Ports embraced the trend whole-heartedly.

I used to joke with folks on tours that I gave that the more extreme the beer, the more popular it was at our place. Not only were people anxious to support local, they were excited to try new and boldly innovative styles. Thus, reason number two: many northlanders love to experiment with new styles and flavors. And with the growing trend in craft beer, people found ample opportunities to satisfy their curiosity.

In the years between 2003 and 2009, great craft beer became a nationwide trend. There was an onslaught of exposure in the media — whether via advertising, business reports, or even crops reports. Print and mass media coverage celebrated the craft-brewing trend along with consumers and brewers alike. A third reason: Lake Superior. Our local beers are made with some of the cleanest, purest water on the planet.

> Beer drinkers in our region loved it. We are very lucky to have such a high concentration of small breweries brewing great beers in our region.

The unique combination of some of the best brewing water on earth, the availability of great ingredients, and the adventuresome attitudes of northern brewers and beer drinkers continued to raise

A pallet of Bent Paddle Brewery's ESB, ready for distribution out of their warehouse in Duluth.

the bar and, in turn, create more demand for new styles, more hops, and more choices. Duluth is well-known in Minnesota as a trend-setting beer destination. It's not just the long winters and the pleasant summers that make Duluth unique. We have a culture in Duluth of seeking out and supporting local businesses. The adage that your neighbor may also be your brewer is strong — and highly likely — in Duluth. Plus, our history is pretty interesting when it comes to brewing.

The history of brewing in the Twin Ports is impressive, but many folks aren't aware of this rich background, and that's because of how far back we have to go. Beer brewing was Duluth's first industry. It started in 1859 when pioneer Sidney Luce financed a brewery built by four unemployed German immigrants. According to Duluth brewing historians Tony Dierckins and Pete Clure:

Roughly a half dozen pioneer brewing operations struggled between economic booms and busts until 1885, when August Fitger and Percy Anneke purchased Mike Fink's Lake Superior Brewery. The Fitger Brewing Company, along with Duluth Brewing & Malting (1895–1966) and People's Brewing Co. (1907–1957), served Duluth during its boom times, struggled through Prohibition, and returned to brewing beer during the Great Depression, but could not survive the post-war consolidation of the brewing industry. When Fitger's stopped brewing in 1972, it marked the end of Duluth's oldest manufacturing business and longest-surviving industry.

(From *Naturally Brewed, Naturally Better: The Historic Breweries of Duluth and Superior.*)

It's remarkable that, after the closing of Fitger's in 1972, there were no breweries in our area until Lake Superior Brewing opened in 1994. After that, Fitger's Brewhouse opened in 1995 as a multi-tap bar while owners built out the brewery. From there, the modern era of brewing in Duluth expanded rapidly. The demand for handcrafted microbrews grew quickly, influenced by the craft beer explosion all around the country.

After 2010, the influx of new, quality breweries like Castle Danger and Bent Paddle — breweries that would eventually distribute their beers outside our area — added more volume to the voice of northern beer.

Looking back at the history of brewing in the 1800s here and comparing it to today's vibrant brewing scene in the Twin Ports really makes me proud. We have this great culture surrounding the craft beer industry — it seems history is truly repeating itself. And in this case, that's a really good thing.

Many longtime brewers in our area cut their teeth at Lake Superior and Fitger's Brewhouse, making every variety possible for northern Minnesota beer-lovers, from wild beers to barrel-aged beers to German-style lagers. Brewers in the Twin Ports also developed a reputation for hoppy beers. The copious use of hops like Cascade, Centennial, and Chinook had been the backbone for the much-loved beers during that initial decade of growth. From these first few small breweries, many veteran brewers opened their own shops and ran with new ideas. Beer drinkers in our region loved it. We are very lucky to have such a high concentration of small breweries brewing great beers in our region.

The range of offerings is bountiful including high quality, high character production breweries like Bent Paddle and Blacklist in Duluth, Castle Danger in Two Harbors, and Earth Rider in Superior. We have wonderful brewpubs like Canal Park Brewery and Fitger's Brewhouse in Duluth, Twin Ports Brewing in Superior, and small nano-breweries like Carmody and Dubh Linn in Duluth, adding brewing to already flourishing bars. We also have a new-style destination beer hall in Hoops Brewing in Canal Park — a small production brewery with a large hall selling most of the beer on site.

Many breweries now offer beer education, tastings, and tours of their facilities. Education of staff has also skyrocketed and the interested beer sampler can usually find out the complete ingredients and beer stats, like color, bitterness level, alcohol level and calorie count. While many breweries offer some groundbreaking brews that push the boundaries of traditional styles, most of the beers we brew are based on age-old styles, some harking back hundreds of years. In each case, the individual brewery puts their own stamp on their interpretation of the style.

I say this a lot, but it remains true: it's a great time to be a beer drinker in the Twin Ports. And that, of course, includes, Duluth, the The Craft Beer Capital of Minnesota (CBC of MN)™. Enjoying quality, handcrafted, homegrown suds brewed with pride by local businesses is at your doorstep here in the Duluth, Superior, and North Shore region. ∎

Dave Hoops has been brewing beer for almost 25 years. Starting out in San Francisco and Chicago, he moved back to Duluth in 1999 and was an integral part of the craft beer surge in the Duluth area. He's also a beer judge, author, and owner of Hoops Brewing in Duluth.

CHAPTER

5

Port Expansion

DULUTH SEAWAY PORT AUTHORITY'S
$18M TERMINAL INVESTMENT SETS STAGE FOR GROWTH

by Jim Sharrow

For well over a century, the Port of Duluth-Superior has been the backbone of this region's economy, anchoring commercial trade and industrial development in Duluth-Superior. However, shifts in trade patterns plus decades of use (and disuse) take a toll on waterfront properties. Thanks to the vision and determination of the Duluth Seaway Port Authority, a vital piece of property on Rice's Point was rehabilitated and put back into maritime service in 2016.

This industrial redevelopment project on Rice's Point was a once-in-a-generation milestone. Breathing new life into a facility that sat idle for 40 years took massive amounts of resources, both human and financial. Converting an unused, unloved 28-acre parcel into a productive,

Cargill C & D facility as it appeared at the time of transfer to the Duluth Seaway Port Authority. Note the curving dirt path (Arthur Avenue) in the lower right corner.

intermodal transport terminal spanned the careers of three port directors, nearly four decades of planning, five federal grant proposals and an infusion of $20 million. And it's been worth every penny.

What is not readily apparent when one drives by the newly minted surface of the pier is the history of the site that once housed 100-year-old grain elevators or the tenacity of the Port Authority's leadership team that brought the project to fruition.

When Davis Helberg became executive director of the Port Authority in 1979, Cargill had just completed the construction of its B1 grain elevator complex further north on Rice's Point. The company's outdated concrete grain elevators C and D on the adjacent property were no longer needed. During the next decade, the Port Authority tried unsuccessfully to help Cargill find a buyer for the property, but the redevelopment costs were daunting.

A decade passed. Unable to find anyone interested in razing the elevators and redeveloping the property, Helberg convinced Cargill to donate the property to the Duluth Seaway Port Authority. Cargill subsequently contributed $50,000 to assist in demolition and site cleanup.

The 1989 transfer of ownership of the C and D pier secured the property in the public domain, keeping it zoned industrial and dedicated to the port's evolving cargo handling needs. As the largest commercial port by tonnage on the Great Lakes by a factor of two, port officials value every dock, every acre of waterfront property adjacent to the harbor's deep draft commercial navigation channel. Once a parcel of land critical to maritime operations is ceded to gentrification, it is nearly impossible to return that tract to industrial redevelopment.

Circling back to the task at hand in 1989, the Port Authority assumed responsibility for redeveloping the former Cargill C and D property. What would be needed? In what order should the work be tackled?

- Two huge 100-year-old grain elevators needed to be razed.

- Dock faces on the south side of Dock "D" and channel dock sides of the property were crumbling and had never been dredged deep enough for modern Seaway-size vessels.

- Legacy contamination existed on the dock and in the adjacent slips.

- Dock "C" had structural issues, but reconstruction could be delayed for a bit.

- Arthur Avenue, a meandering dirt trail that flooded during parts of the year, ended at the dock entrance and was not connected to Port Terminal Drive. A new road to serve all maritime facilities on Rice's Point was needed — one that would connect with Port Terminal Drive and Garfield Avenue — the genesis of what is now Helberg Drive.

Elevators were partially dismantled using dynamite and then removed using mechanical means.

RAZING THE GRAIN ELEVATORS

With a State of Minnesota grant in hand to support removal of the two grain elevators, the Port Authority contracted with Duluth engineering firm LHB in the mid-1990s to prepare plans and bid specifications for razing the structures. It would take two different contractors to complete the demolition process. By 2001, the dock faces were once again useable for ship repairs and winter layup, though no cargo could be transferred. Great Lakes Towing leased part of the facility for their tugs. The property was renamed Garfield C & D.

HELBERG DRIVE CONSTRUCTION

Next on the checklist was constructing a new road to replace the meandering dirt trail known as Arthur Avenue. Construction plans and bidding specifications were developed by Duluth engineering firm SEH, under contract with the Port Authority, which then contracted with the City of Duluth to receive a grant from the Federal Highway Administration. That was made possible by including the project in the Metropolitan Interstate Council's Transportation Improvement Plan. The Port Authority leveraged the federal grant with funds from MnDOT's Port Development Assistance Program (PDAP) and its own capital investment to build the $5.8-million road. Construction required a complex assemblage of parcels. Approximately half the cost was spent rearranging the Canadian Pacific main line and yard as well as the BNSF Railway main line on Rice's Point.

The project, completed in 2007, created excellent road access with direct connections to both Port Terminal Drive and Garfield Avenue for all industrial and maritime property owners and tenants on Rice's Point. The Port Authority's Clure Public Marine Terminal could now enjoy two-way

> The project was the largest and most expensive since the completion of the original Arthur M. Clure Public Marine Terminal in 1958. It took years of faith, a marathon of planning and an influx of hard-earned capital to bring this project to fruition.

access to Garfield Avenue and to I-35. The Port Authority's terminal operator, Lake Superior Warehousing, invested in re-grading the Garfield C & D site to allow for additional outdoor storage areas for equipment and cargo. The historic Canadian Pacific and BNSF rail connections to the facility were not replaced during this phase of construction. That would have to wait for the next stage of redevelopment.

Workers complete final preparations before concrete placement for the new heavy lift dock in June 2016.

A TIGER "IN OUR TANK"
Transportation Infrastructure Generating Economic Revitalization

The federal TIGER grant program was initiated by Congress during the Obama administration in 2009. Tied to congressional efforts to help the American economy recover from the Great Recession, states and localities competed for infrastructure funding, albeit limited. The TIGER program typically offered just $600 million to $1 billion in grants but received project proposals for nearly $20 billion each year. Obviously, only the best planned, shovel-ready projects with the highest return on federal investment could win one of these grants, and the percentage awarded to maritime projects across the country was quite small.

Photo by Dennis O'Hara/Northern Images Photography

Construction work was completed in October, 2016. Note the paved Helberg Drive *(noted in story/constructed in 2007).*

FIFTH TIME'S A CHARM

The Duluth Seaway Port Authority applied for TIGER grants in 2009, 2010, 2011 and 2012 to reconstruct the berths and slip at the Garfield C & D property. Each year, our project made it to the last round of finalists, only to be cut days before grants were announced. Quite honestly, after being turned down in 2012, Port Authority staff concluded that any further applications would be a waste of time.

Shortly after the announcement of another round of TIGER grants in 2013, Mayor Don Ness called Adolph Ojard, then Port Authority executive director, urging him to apply a fifth time. Ness had heard from sources in Washington that they hoped Duluth would apply again. The project to redevelop Garfield C & D was titled *"The Port of Duluth Intermodal Facility.*" The scope of work was pared down from prior applications to support what was estimated to be a $16 million project (realizing that some of the desired work would need to be postponed).

The formula worked, and the Port Authority was awarded a $10-million TIGER grant. Coupled with $2.75 million in state PDAP funds, a $990,000 contamination cleanup grant from the Department of Employment and Economic Development (DEED) and $4 million of Port Authority capital, funding was in place to finally redevelop the property. The project's price tag, which eventually grew to $17.7 million after final engineering was completed, became the largest and most expensive project to be undertaken by the Duluth Seaway Port Authority since the completion of the original Arthur M. Clure Public Marine Terminal in 1958.

THE CONSTRUCTION PROCESS

Notice of the TIGER grant award in the fall of 2013 initiated a year-long final engineering design process under the Port Authority's new executive director, Vanta E. Coda II. Duluth firm LHB was contracted to provide the overall engineering design process. Sub-contractors included Barr Engineering for environmental design and preparation of the Remediation Action Plan and AMI Consulting Engineers to prepare the structural design and dredging specifications. Separately, Krech Ojard & Associates was contracted to perform project construction administration. Lunda Construction Co. of Black River Falls, Wis., won the bid and was hired as general contractor.

Work commenced in April 2015, and an official groundbreaking was held on May 27. The project was completed in October 2016. The renovated facility has since been renamed the Clure Public Marine Terminal Expansion. Dock sections were renamed, too, as the letters "C" and "D" no longer had a frame of reference. Today, the berths are numbered consecutively, starting with berths 8 and 9 along the inner and outer halves of the south dock wall. The short, outer end of the dock — next up for renovation — is now berth 10, while the far north edge of the pier is berth 11. At the inner end of berth 8 is a new roll-on/roll-off dock.

NUTS AND BOLTS

New steel sheet piling was driven along approximately 1,700 feet of dock wall, forming berths 8 and 9. The upper portions of all steel sheet piles were epoxy-coated to protect them from an accelerated corrosion problem prevalent in this harbor. Steel pilings that support the roll-on/roll-off dock were similarly coated. That dock plus berths 8 and 9 are designed to support a surface load of 2,000 pounds per square foot — twice what any berth at the 1958 terminal can hold. The roll-on/roll-off dock is supported by pilings above the water surface — allowing fish and other wildlife access to the watery world below. This resolved a concern by the Minnesota DNR that could have imposed a mitigation requirement for the loss of open water habitat.

Approximately 63,000 cubic yards of sediment were dredged from the slip. All but 500 cubic yards of material met MPCA standards for re-use in residential areas and was placed in several locations by Veit, the dredging sub-contractor. About a third of the material was shared by two brownfield sites owned by the City—the Atlas Cement site in Morgan Park and the former DWP rail roundhouse site in West Duluth. The balance was used to help close two gravel pits outside city limits. Contaminated soils and sediment were removed and properly land-filled.

Eventually, the pier's surface was re-graded to direct rainwater to a new storm water drainage system. A new shared rail turn-out was built from the Canadian Pacific rail yard across Helberg Drive, enabling switching agreements to remain in place with both Canadian Pacific and BNSF Railway. Security fencing, fire hydrants, a guard shack and outdoor lighting fixtures were incorporated into the final project design.

At the time of this writing (2018), berths 8 and 9 are busy hosting domestic freighters and foreign ships, and the refurbished dock surface is filling up fast with wind turbine components and other power plant equipment being stored/staged in Duluth for energy projects across the Heartland. The Port Authority also is in the midst of designing a second phase: reconstruction and dredging of berth 10 at the outer end of the pier.

A section of the rehabbed dock was immediately used for storage/staging of wind turbine components.

ANOTHER CENTURY OF SERVICE

Federal and state support and the patience and persistence of the Duluth Seaway Port Authority across 30-plus years and the careers of three executive directors, resulted in the rehabilitation of an important structure on the deep federal navigation channel in the Duluth-Superior Harbor. Not only did the redevelopment project re-establish the dock's structural integrity, but it also connected the site to new, improved road and rail infrastructure.

It took years of faith, a marathon of planning and an influx of hard-earned capital to bring this project to fruition. One director's vision

Photo by Dennis O'Hara/Northern Images Photography

and optimism set the wheels in motion. Thank you, Davis Helberg. Another director's tenacity to apply five times for a TIGER grant paid off. Kudos, Adolph Ojard. And a final word of thanks to the director who carried the mantle forward — to Vanta Coda who shepherded the project through its design and construction phases — moving the working waterfront toward its next century of service. This port, after all, is the "Pride of the Inland Seas." We celebrate our maritime heritage and are grateful to have helped set the stage for the port's future growth. ∎

Steve Isola

Jim Sharrow retired in April 2018 from the Duluth Seaway Port Authority after 15 years of service. Having joined the staff as facilities manager, he was later named director of port planning and resiliency and was responsible for overseeing the organization's capital program, maritime policy, risk management and security plans, plus its connectivity to regional planning initiatives. Sharrow, who has a degree in naval architecture and marine engineering from the University of Michigan, spent the first 28 years of his career with Duluth-based Great Lakes Fleet.

AUTHOR ACKNOWLEDGMENTS

AMI Consulting Engineers P.A.	Structural design, dredging specifications, assistance with environmental permitting
Barr Engineering	Environmental design & Remediation Action Plan preparation
Belknap Electric	Area lighting, guard shack power
Braun Intertec	Remediation Action Plan final report, pile driving reports, material testing
CP Rail	Installation of rail switch
Duluth Ready Mix	Concrete supply
EBI, Inc.	Utility boring, installation
IDS, Inc.	Welded modifications to sheet piling
Krech Ojard & Associates, Inc.	Project construction administration
LHB	Lead design engineer, civil engineering design, preparation of construction specifications
Lunda Construction Co.	General contractor
North Shore Track	Rail construction
Mavo Systems	Concrete boring and sawing
Nordic Group	Inspections, underwater storm sewer construction, submerged debris removal
Northern Interstate Construction	Earthwork, fill materials, grading
Quality Sandblasting & Coatings	Steel coatings
SEH	Rail design
Sherwin-Williams	Paint products and testing
Stonebrook Fence	Security fencing
Veit	Disposal of contaminated materials, dredging

LEGACY ISSUES

*"We cannot solve our problems
with the same level of thinking
that created them."*

—Albert Einstein

CHAPTER

6

Eliminating Sanitary Sewer Overflows

PROTECTING LAKE SUPERIOR, OUR MOST SACRED RESPONSIBILITY

by Kurt Soderberg

Eliminating sanitary sewer overflows may not sound like an alluring topic, but it's a critical part of our community's most important environmental success story of the past 30 years: the cleanup of the St. Louis River. For decades, citizens knew that manholes, pump stations, and the treatment plant were spilling sewage during the spring snowmelt and during big rain events. Citizens of Duluth and surrounding communities faced substantial changes necessary to tackle this environmental problem. Changes, large and small, would ultimately extend right into people's homes.

The cleanup of the St. Louis River is largely attributed to the creation of the Western Lake Superior Sanitary District (WLSSD), a regional wastewater collection and treatment

Steve Forslund, City of Duluth

Steve Forslund, City of Duluth

Lakeside Interceptor Basin 2, both under construction by the City of Duluth and in its final form. This basin is at about 20th Avenue East, adjacent to the Lakewalk. It will hold up to 3 million gallons of sewage and works in conjunction with another tank holding 1 million gallons just two blocks to the west, toward downtown. Above ground, it serves to provide parking for Lakewalk users.

system created by state statute in the early 1970s. Following the startup of the WLSSD, and the buy-in and tie-in of 17 area communities and five major industries, the water quality in the St. Louis River improved significantly. This improvement meant that people could use the river again and that significantly cleaner river water flowed into Lake Superior.

While the creation of the WLSSD was vital to water quality improvement, issues remained when excessive rainfall overflowed the sanitary sewer collection systems in Duluth and surrounding communities — an issue not unique to our region, but unacceptable, nonetheless. Resolving this persistent problem required region-wide dedication, cooperation and creativity. It required citizens from Duluth, Hermantown, Cloquet, and other surrounding communities to get on board in a collective effort — investment in community infrastructure via rate increases and (in some cases, major) improvements to private home systems would be pivotal in fixing the problem.

Two distinctly different underground sewer systems serve most communities in this area: one handles wastewater from homes and businesses, and the other handles stormwater from rainfall and runoff. A pipe called a lateral line connects each home to the sanitary sewer pipe beneath the street. Wastewater travels from the lateral line to the sanitary sewer. Then it merges into larger and larger pipes as it travels down the streets, and ultimately into the WLSSD wastewater treatment plant at 27th Avenue West in Duluth. The sewage is treated and discharged into the St. Louis River. Meanwhile, stormwater systems move rainwater into larger and larger connector pipes and ultimately send it back into the streams and lakes. When rainwater flows into the sanitary sewer system rather than into the stormwater system, it is called inflow and infiltration, I&I, for short. Heavy rainfall events often quadrupled I&I volume, compared to normal daily volume, and understandably overwhelmed the system.

Any raw sewage entering our fresh waters is too much. But the relatively infrequent, short-term I&I peak didn't warrant a sewer system re-build, which would have been infeasible. In other words, sewer pipes and a treatment plant large enough to successfully handle these rain events without overflowing would be way too large and expensive for everyday use.

Beginning in the early 1990s, the City of Duluth and WLSSD teamed up in a concerted effort to eliminate sewer overflows. The first step was to pinpoint the I&I cause(s), or places within the system where clear water entered the sanitary sewer. The investigation identified two major I&I causes. The first: old, leaky sewer pipes let in substantial amounts of groundwater (infiltration). The second: broken lateral lines, and faulty foundation drains and downspouts — private, residential infrastructure — similarly allowed groundwater to leak into the sewer system (inflow). A series of neighborhood meetings gathered citizens to learn about the problem and hopefully energize people to initiate home improvement in support of fixing the problem.

> Resolving this persistent problem required region-wide dedication, cooperation and creativity. It required citizens from Duluth, Hermantown, Cloquet, and other surrounding communities to get on board in a collective effort.

WLSSD and the city began replacing, cleaning, and patching leaky sewer pipes. Meanwhile, the inflow from residential infrastructure continued.

Duluth City Council passed an ordinance in 1994 in an attempt to curb the inflow issue. The ordinance required every home in Duluth have a sump pump that discharged to the outside of the house, allowing groundwater to drain naturally back into the ground. Controversy surrounding this ordinance led to its repeal but prompted creation of a task force to address the inflow problem.

The task force's arduous, honorable effort produced a program concept that targeted neighborhoods with high inflow rates and provided the neighborhoods' homeowners help with foundation drain disconnects and sump pump installation. These changes helped, but sewer overflows persisted. The program grew to include other elements, such as better maintenance plans for pumps, sewers, control systems, and cleaning, both in WLSSD's system and the city's.

Progress continued through the 1990s and early 2000s. By this time, both WLSSD and the City of Duluth had planned and begun to build a series of large, underground storage tanks to capture overflow in high-volume areas. Though the new program had significantly diminished overflows, the springtime snowmelt continued to overwhelm the system every year.

In April of 2003, a succession of unlucky events stormed WLSSD's system. First, a pipe joint near the paper mill in Cloquet corroded, failed, and dumped out paper-mill wastewater. That summer, heavy rainstorms, power failures at pumping stations, and control system failures resulted in a slew of overflows. The setback accentuated the problem, and more importantly, the need to solve it. Citizens demanded action; the Environmental Protection Agency (EPA) and the Minnesota Pollution Control Agency (MPCA) noticed.

> After seven years of effort, WLSSD, the City of Duluth, citizens and our other municipal and industrial partners in the region satisfied consent decree requirements a year ahead of schedule.

WLSSD installed backup generators at each of its pumping stations and the main treatment plant that very year — a step not required by regulators in the past. Now pumping stations and the treatment

Steve Forslund, City of Duluth

Steve Forslund, City of Duluth

The largest sewer overflow tank, under construction then complete, adjacent to Canal Park and Lakeplace Park. This largest tank will hold up to 8.3 million gallons of sewage that may have otherwise overflowed into Lake Superior or onto local streets. This is the final piece of a series of five tanks stretching from 60th Avenue East and London Road to this tank downtown. Above ground, it serves as additional park and viewing space.

plant would continue operating through any power outage.

The EPA and MPCA began a process that ended in a legally binding agreement called a consent decree in 2004. The consent decree established a checklist Duluth and WLSSD needed to fulfill, and the organizations' legal arms — U.S. Department of Justice (for the EPA) and the Minnesota Attorney General's office (for the MPCA) — enforced the criteria it laid out. The list identified 17 overflow points and required their full compliance, meaning overflow elimination, by 2016.

A signed consent decree in October of 2008 set in motion a more rigorous plan to eliminate sanitary sewer overflows in our community. An I&I reduction ordinance mandated all communities in the WLSSD system follow an I&I elimination plan; the City of Duluth formalized sump pump installation and lateral line replacement grants to assist homeowners with upgrades necessary to meet new standards; the city and WLSSD invested in a total of eight overflow storage basins, including those installed prior to the consent decree.

Work began. Homeowners installed sump pumps and replaced or repaired their lateral lines; the city fixed, lined, and replaced more old sewer pipes; maintenance crews moved forward with better practices. It wasn't simply an engineering project, digging up pipes and fixing them. It was a region-wide effort that affected entire neighborhoods as numerous homes underwent significant repair and upgrades, and as citizens learned

Storage basins constructed *BEFORE* the consent decree:

WLSSD constructed a one-million-gallon storage basin in 2003 in Gary/New Duluth (the only one with an open top and above ground) that effectively stopped overflows in that area.

The City of Duluth followed in 2005, constructing a nearly-two-million-gallon underground tank at 52nd Avenue East and Dodge Street, a 300,000-gallon underground tank the following year at 60th Avenue East at Lake Superior, and a one-million-gallon underground tank in 2007 at 18th Avenue East and the Lakewalk.

Storage basins constructed *AFTER* the consent decree:

The City of Duluth built a three-million-gallon tank in 2010 at 20th Avenue East and Water Street, and an unprecedented eight-million-gallon+ tank in 2011 at the corner of the Lakeplace Park.

Also in 2011, WLSSD built a one-million-gallon tank underground in West Duluth, just off of Central Avenue and Polk Street near the paper mill, and a small tank near Pike Lake. ∎

how to reduce the amount of ground water getting into sanitary sewer systems. And soon those sources where clear water once entered the sewer system greatly diminished.

The new storage basins, which hold and control the release of excess flow to prevent collection pipes and the treatment facility from backing up, emerged across Duluth. All of these tanks comprise nearly 17 million gallons of storage capacity for sanitary sewer overflow — overflow that would have otherwise entered the streets, streams, the St. Louis River, and Lake Superior.

In the summer of 2015, after seven years of effort, WLSSD, the City of Duluth, citizens and our other municipal and industrial partners in the region satisfied consent decree requirements a year ahead of schedule. More importantly, Duluth and our neighbors have virtually eliminated sanitary sewer overflows. That's a testament to our community's will, our power in public and private collaboration, and our environmental stewardship. The St. Louis River, our many other rivers and streams, and Lake Superior reap the hard-earned benefits, and therefore, so do we. ∎

Kurt Soderberg retired in 2008 as the executive director of the Western Lake Superior Sanitary District (WLSSD), serving as such for 17 years. He was born and raised in Ely, MN and moved to Duluth in 1970, where he graduated from UMD with a master's degree in psychology. He was involved with many organizations and task forces related to Lake Superior and water and wastewater issues in Minnesota and also on a national level.

AUTHOR ACKNOWLEDGMENTS

The author gratefully acknowledges the assistance of Marianne Bohren and Jack Ezell from WLSSD, and Eric Shaffer and Howard Smith of the City of Duluth.

CHAPTER

7

Solving Retiree Health Care Crisis

CITIZEN-LED EFFORT TO FORESTALL CITY'S FINANCIAL RUIN

by Arend "Sandy" Sandbulte

I received a call in the summer of 2005 from then-president of the Duluth City Council, Don Ness, who asked me to attend a noon meeting in the lower level of the old Duluth Athletic Club. Ness gave no hint of the purpose of the meeting, other than it involved a matter important to Duluth.

I showed up at the meeting to find, in addition to Ness, attorneys Don Bye and John Nys, insurance agents Dave Lindstrom and Al Winters, and St. Scholastica PhD economist and professor Bob Hoffman.

Ness explained the purpose of the meeting briefly. A recent actuarial study had estimated the City of Duluth's unfunded retiree health care liability, relating to its then-current benefit plans with no actual funding source, had reached $280 million on January 1, 2005. Further, this immense liability was increasing rapidly. With medical

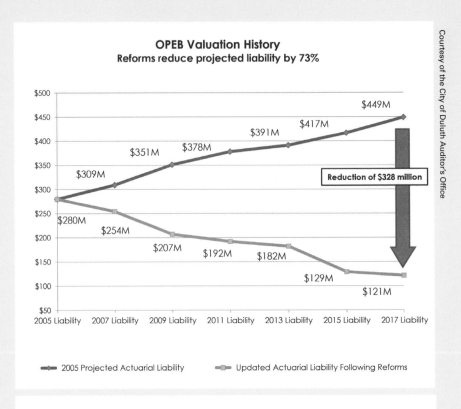

The difference between $449M and $121M is the difference between eventual bankruptcy and solvency.

costs predicted to outrun U.S. inflation rates, the actuary firm projected the City's unfunded liability would reach $350 million in just five years and over $400 million in nine years.

The Governmental Accounting Standards Board (GASB) had recently prescribed new accounting and financial reporting requirements for Post Employment Benefits other than Pensions (OPEB). GASB was determined to provide current and future investors, and anyone interested in the financial health of cities and other governmental units, with the true financial status of those entities. The City of Duluth had to take a long-overdue look at its OPEB practices and liabilities.

At Ness's request, Hoffman had completed an initial analysis and comparison of the City's OPEB status, which together with the actuarial study, confirmed Duluth had a *big* problem – bigger, in absolute terms, than any other municipality in Minnesota, and in relative terms, one of the worst in the country. This problem had been known for some time in City Hall but had apparently been wished to somehow eventually disappear. Without a solution, the City's bonds would most likely be downgraded below investment-grade, which would prompt much higher interest rates and potential insolvency.

Ness suggested that the five citizens called in for lunch that day undertake as a volunteer task force the deeper study and resolution of the elephantine problem he had laid out. We unanimously committed, not knowing the full scope of the charge but willing to give it a shot. I accepted the invitation to chair the task force. Later that summer the City Council unanimously approved the membership and mission of the Task Force. With Council's blessing, the Task Force began meeting weekly in City Hall, getting our heads and arms around the complex problem.

Our goal was to present a final report to the Council in December of that year. Certain realities became inarguably clear at the outset: the unfunded liability had to be addressed in its entirety; leaving any piece of the liability without resolution would recreate the same issue down the road; and no single action by the Council or the City would even come close to solving the problem — multiple steps would be required.

I was keenly aware of the financial implications of unfunded liability resulting from promised benefits. In the private sector, efforts never cease to ensure assets held in trust fully fund the promised benefits to employees and retirees. Any underfunding is typically temporary, nominal, and not allowed to persist. Annual financial reports to shareholders and regulators point out funding shortfalls, and investors notice looming financial problems. But the City of Duluth's unfunded retiree health care liability had largely gone unnoticed to this point — at least the magnitude of which — and had certainly come as a surprise to me.

We learned that the City had been promising its employees retirement benefits which current financial plans didn't adequately fund. The City had instead adopted a pay-as-you-go approach to managing retiree health care benefits, essentially covering costs incurred each year without regard to the factors that were driving those costs: the number of active employees relative to retirees was shrinking; retirees were living longer; technology and efficiency improvements gave way to a leaner active workforce.

The effect was similar to the familiar national social security story: a smaller workforce supported a burgeoning number of retirees. The result? A huge funding problem. So the City, instead of putting away money to pay future benefits, was simply paying out whatever came in through employee and retiree health care payments withheld from their paychecks and taxpayer funds. "Live for today and let tomorrow take care of itself" seemed to be the thinking, if not specifically, then in actual effect.

To illustrate the relationship of out-of-pocket costs versus what should be booked per GASB's new rules: the actual amount paid out by the City for medical claims in 2005 was $6.8 million; the amount GASB prescribed should be set aside that year in order to cover current costs and amortize the unfunded liability over 30 years was $26 million; so the true cost of retiree medical plans for 2005 was 3.8 times as much as the City had made provision for. Stated another way, in 2005 the City was providing only 26% of the true cost, over the long term, of its promised benefits. Clearly, the path the City was on would eventually lead to huge financial shortfalls.

The Task Force studied possible solutions, which over 30 years, would eliminate completely the current actuarial deficit of $280 million (growing by leaps and bounds every year).

The Task Force determined early on that an effective solution required higher co-pays and deductibles for retirees — understandably, not a popular idea amongst retirees. They believed they were entitled to the same medical plan which existed on the date of their retirement. To satisfy that position alone implied the City would need to maintain a multitude of different plans — a practice neither efficient nor sustainable — since plans changed regularly during labor negotiations and new contract agreements. Over the years, the City's health care benefits had remained highly competitive when compared to the greater community. Active employees' plans had seen enhanced benefits, like higher lifetime limits and expanded coverage. And along with those enhancements (and rising health care costs), co-pays and deductibles increased incrementally. The enhancements had been passed along to retirees as well, while co-pay and deductible increases had *not*. The Task Force described retirees' benefits as "the best of both worlds" — improving benefits at a fixed lower cost.

The Task Force reviewed labor contracts, which ultimately did not support retirees' entitlement to the *same* medical plans as they existed the day of individual retirements. Labor contracts supported equal co-pay and deductible increases for active and retired employees alike.

The Task Force members remained true to our original commitment despite steep demands on our time and daunting political pressure. We volunteered hundreds of hours to studying this issue and laying out every possible factor for deliberation.

The changes in retiree health care plans were the most important piece in the jigsaw puzzle of financial viability for the City of Duluth, but there were many other important steps. Among them: improved administrative efficiencies; importation of prescription drugs; local property tax increases; and establishing a trust fund to hold funds generated or saved to meet future years' OPEB requirements. True to our initial goal, the Task Force laid out 15 recommendations to the Council in December 2005, proposing complete elimination of the City's OPEB unfunded liability over the 30-year period promulgated by GASB. The Council voted unanimously in favor of the Task Force's report in its entirety and instructed the City administration to move forward with implementation.

Some retiree groups fought tooth and toenail against the City's decision to move them to the health care plans for active employees. The City prevailed at the end of a several-year deliberation, which included litigation. Ultimately, a court ruling supported the City's consolidation of retiree health care plans, thanks in large part to

Ness (who was mayor by then) and his determination to solve the problem of unfunded health care liability.

Mayor Ness deemed retiree health care liability one of the biggest threats to the financial viability of our city government and upheld its reform as one of the most significant successes of his administration. He has characterized the work of the Task Force this way: "It's likely the most important volunteer effort in our city's history — it saved us from bankruptcy."

Fast forward to 2018, 13 years after the Task Force's work was completed and its final report approved unanimously by the City Council. The latest actuarial study determined the current unfunded liability for health plans at the end of 2015 was $129 million, less than half of the $280 million of ten years prior and less than one-third of the projected number for 2015 ($417 million if nothing had been done). The City established a trust fund for retiree health care benefits as recommended by the Task Force, which now has a balance of about $50 million. This represents substantial progress: $280 million shrinking to $129 million over a period of ten years. ∎

Arend "Sandy" Sandbulte chaired the City of Duluth Task Force on funding post retirement health care benefits in 2005. Prior to this work, Sandbulte retired as chairman, president and CEO of Minnesota Power (now ALLETE) in 1996 after 31 years and continued serving its board until 2002. He's served his community via membership on numerous boards, including as chair in many cases, and his country via service in the United States Army.

CHAPTER

8

St. Louis River Estuary

AGGRESSIVE REHAB FOR AN ABUSED WATERWAY

by William "Bill" Majewski

THE PROBLEM

The Twin Ports' natural environment has paid a cost for its prosperous industrial past. Contamination lies below the surface in various parts of our city, and we've made a concerted effort to clean up the mess over the last several decades. One place affected heavily by old industrial practices is the largest tributary feeding Lake Superior on the U.S. side: the St. Louis River. The river begins its course near Hoyt Lakes, MN, and travels nearly 200 miles to its terminus at Lake Superior. A 12,000-acre freshwater estuary marks the confluence of the river and lake. The lower part of the estuary is home to the Twin Ports' urban development, industrial harbor and port.

Sawmilling in the early 1900s followed by steel manufacturing and other industrial operations near the waterfront contaminated the St. Louis River. In fact,

Lyell Brand, United Northern Sportsmen president in the 1950s poking floating sludge on the St. Louis River.

dumping industrial waste directly into the river was commonplace. On top of that, municipal sanitary waste received only minimal treatment before its disposal into the river at multiple locations between Cloquet, Gary-New Duluth and Downtown Duluth. One example was in the Fond du Lac area of Duluth where sanitary sewage drains emptied into the nearest ditch, if not directly into the river. Such neglectful, and perhaps partly ignorant, use of the St. Louis River and Lake Superior carried on for several decades.

This scenario played out similarly in waterway cities across our country as industry expanded and buoyed local economies and populations grew. A commonly referenced event occurred in 1969 in Ohio, when a spark from a passing train near the Republic Steel Mill caused an oil slick on the Cuyahoga River to catch fire, resulting in more than $2 million in damage, largely to two highway bridges. Although fires like this one occasionally happened in other industrial cities, the Cuyahoga River fire became the symbol of out-of-control waterway pollution and ultimately inspired Congress to take action.

LEGISLATION AND GROUNDWORK

Over the few years following the Cuyahoga River fire, Congress enacted legislation called the Clean Water Act, adopted in 1972 as an amendment to the 1948 Federal Water Pollution Control Act. The Clean Water Act designated funding to help implement new standards at the local level.

Willard Munger served as a Minnesota state representative for the western portion of Duluth at the time. The river's condition had long concerned him. In addition to its unpleasant smell and floating waste, the water was continually contaminated by chemical waste from the paper mill and steel mills located upstream. The river certainly didn't lend itself to recreation or healthy enjoyment anymore. Its wildlife had drastically dwindled, and the remaining fish were no longer suitable for eating. Willard, who proudly wore the "Mr. Environment" label in the legislature, led several unsuccessful attempts to establish the Western Lake Superior Sanitary District (WLSSD), proposed to encompass a 500-square-mile area on the Minnesota side of the river between Duluth and Cloquet. The WLSSD's charge would be to effectively manage wastewater and further protect and preserve the quality of the St. Louis River. With encouragement from the United Northern Sportsmen, a Minnesota conservation club, and under the tutelage of Alden Lind, longtime advocate for protecting and conserving Lake Superior, Willard persisted.

The WLSSD was established in 1971. A year passed before federal legislation provided funding needed to develop the WLSSD and construct the infrastructure to reroute the industrial and sanitary waste streams from eighteen different locations into an effective single treatment facility.

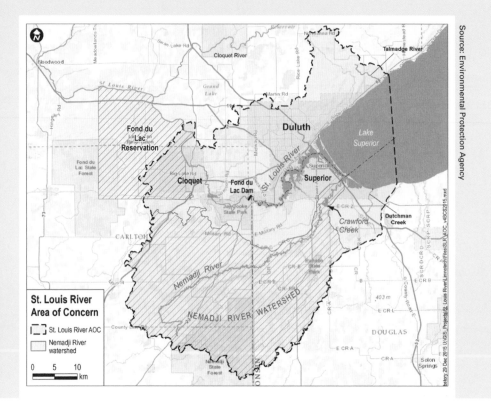

By 1978 (seven years and over $100 million of federal assistance later), the treatment facility and collection system went on line. This marked the elimination of point source discharges, places where wastewater had directly entered the river. Within a relatively short time, the stench on the water began to disappear and users began to venture onto the river once again. But under the cleaned water's surface, polluted sediment remained and needed the public's attention and action.

COMMUNITY ENGAGEMENT

The Great Lakes Water Quality Agreement (GLWQA), established in 1972 between the United States and Canada, aims to restore and protect the waters of the Great Lakes. It provides a framework for identifying bi-national priorities and implementing actions to improve water quality. The GLWQA designated the St. Louis

River estuary an official Area of Concern (AOC) in 1987. An AOC is defined as a place "where significant impairment of beneficial uses has occurred as a result of human activities," or a place that has experienced environmental degradation.

At a public meeting at Denfeld High School in 1988, the International Joint Commission (IJC), charged with administering the GLWQA, announced the AOC designation and charged state and local officials with developing a remedial action plan (RAP) for the estuary. The long-term goal: delist the estuary.

The RAP process would require participation from the states of Minnesota and Wisconsin, the cities of Duluth and Superior, and the Fond du Lac Tribe. Setting up shared leadership and a work plan didn't come easily. But eventually the two states jointly provided staffing, and work began.

With the IJC's framework in hand, people began organizing around the charge. Anyone interested in the issue was welcome and encouraged to participate in the process. Roughly 200-300 people — including people from higher education, and local, tribal, county, state and federal agencies — showed up to take part in the early conversations. The groups identified nine specific problems, called beneficial use impairments, afflicting our part of the estuary:

- fish consumption advisories,
- degraded fish and wildlife populations,
- fish tumors and other deformities,
- degradation of benthos,
- restrictions on dredging,
- excessive loading of sediment and nutrients (discovered by our community, not an item on the national list of identified impairments),
- beach closings and body contact restrictions,
- degradation of aesthetics, and
- loss of fish and wildlife habitat.

St. Louis River Alliance

Initial gathering of resource managers to begin mapping out Habitat Plan development; other managers attended but are not pictured.

Front: Rick Gitar, Larry Schwarzkopf, Paul Sandstrom; Back: Dave Warburton, Bill Majewski, Pat Collins, Carl Richards, Fred Strand.

The list prompted scientific assessment in each category and subsequent development of remedial steps. Agencies pivotal in this process included Minnesota and Wisconsin Departments of Natural Resources (DNR) and the Minnesota Pollution Control Agency (MPCA).

The first stage RAP was submitted to the IJC in 1992, and its second stage, in 1995. Then in 2002, the Habitat Plan was completed, funded by a grant from the U.S. Environmental Protection Agency (EPA) and support from the Minnesota DNR, U.S. Fish and Wildlife Service (FWS), and The Nature Conservancy. The Habitat

Plan identified threats to the lower St. Louis River and strategies for addressing them. It has since served as a model for the other Great Lakes AOC sites.

The RAP's were staffed by Nancy Larson of Wisconsin DNR and Brian Frederickson of MPCA. The Habitat Plan was the result of collaboration by the St. Louis River Alliance, formerly St. Louis River Citizen's Action Committee, which included Karen Plass, Lynelle Hanson, Julene Boe, Bill Majewski; Tom Duffus of The Nature Conservancy; Pat Collins, John Lindgren, Rich Staffon, and Martha Minchak of Minnesota DNR; Fred Strand and Ted Smith of Wisconsin DNR; Rick Gitar and Nancy Schult of the Fond du Lac Reservation; Dave Warburton of U.S. FWS; Jane Anklam of NW Wisconsin Land Trust; Jesse Schomberg of Minnesota Sea Grant; Jack Ezell of WLSSD; and many others.

The truly remarkable part of this story is the community's stewardship, which sparked a massive, collective effort to heal our environment — hundreds of people claiming the problem as their own, committing to stay the course to restore our stretch of the St. Louis River.

The St. Louis River Alliance (SLRA, originally the St. Louis River Citizen's Action Committee) formed primarily as a liaison between public and tribal entities, industrial groups, and the community in the mission to develop and implement RAP's, and ultimately restore, protect, and enhance the St. Louis River. The SLRA facilitated the group effort to develop criteria for delisting the St.

Louis River estuary. These criteria served as tools to measure the effectiveness of remedial work. Considerable public participation proved instrumental in establishing a new set of standards by which we hoped to recover our river's vitality.

Planning and work to clean up petroleum-based contaminants at Newton Creek and Hog Island Inlet (near the Wisconsin side of the harbor) spanned the decade between 1995 and 2005. This project was accomplished under the direction of Wisconsin DNR with funding arranged through the State of Wisconsin.

In 2005, a community work group took up resolution of PCB contamination, which the MPCA identified back in 1979, at the InterLake Iron site. The work group included neighborhood residents and local chapter Izaak Walton League members. Within five years, the group's remedial plan, led by the MPCA, guided complete underwater cleanup at InterLake Iron. The work group received a "Partnership Minnesota" award from the Governor for their work, which contributed to the protection and conservation of Stryker Bay.

The U.S. Steel site in Morgan Park is considered the other half of the InterLake Iron sediment cleanup project. The U.S. Steel part would be placed on hold to allow the navigation of the project's multiple complexities. Similarity in contaminants made the InterLake project a potential guide for the eventual U.S. Steel site cleanup. Given the magnitude and complexity of this effort, the GLRI offered funding to incentivize the initiation of work. Preparation began in 2014 and is ongoing.

In 2008, Minnesota voters supported a constitutional amendment titled the "Clean Water, Land and Legacy Amendment," which dedicated a 3/8ths of one percent sales tax to outdoor programs and projects for a 25-year span. The amendment makes available about $80 million per year to support projects such as AOC cleanup. This statewide effort was co-led by David Zentner, active with the Izaak Walton League for many years, along with other outdoor and environmental groups.

ACTION

Those several years of collaboration between multiple agencies and the community laid important groundwork for a new federal initiative in 2010, which would accelerate restoration efforts. The Great Lakes Restoration Initiative (GLRI) allotted Clean Water Act funding matches for Great Lakes projects, thereby ushering in a new government funding stream for projects, which had, up to this point, been largely funded privately. For the last several years, Congress has appropriated about $300 million per year for Great Lakes projects.

GLRI funding allowed RAP updates, which in 2013 became the "Roadmap to Delisting," a program to systematically cleanup contaminated sites — 60+ projects to be completed by 2020. The state's Clean Water Act funding matches would leverage local and federal dollars. Nelson French of the MPCA played a major role in plan development. The plan projected delisting by 2025.

To date, projects large and small dot the timeline to delisting. Projects tend to include habitat restoration alongside the contamination cleanup — this is true throughout the estuary, and especially in the lower area affected most severely by industrial activities.

- Shoreline stabilization and fortification at Interstate Island in 2015 enhanced the nesting habitat for terns.

- U.S. FWS funded improvement of nesting habitat for the piping plover on Wisconsin and Minnesota Point beaches from 2010 to 2017. SLRA coordinated the work with the Cities of Duluth and Superior and Douglas County.

- Tower Bay, a former sawmill site, was cleaned up in 2015. The wood waste harvested from the site was ground up into slurry, which was pumped to the U.S. Steel site for use in future cleanup projects.

- The Pier B development project on the downtown waterfront in 2015-16 helped fund cleanup and stabilization of the slip adjacent the $20+ million resort hotel construction.

Hansi Johnson

Today's St. Louis River estuary is a sanctuary for paddlers, fishers, water-lovers of all kinds.

- In 2016, the State of Minnesota funded aquatic invasive species management. The SLRA received grants under this program to provide education to waterway users to identify invasive plants and effectively remove Phragmites from the shoreline.

- Thanks to private funding and GLRI dollars, work began in 2017 to clean up the contaminated slip at Howards Pocket, adjacent Fraser Shipyard on the Wisconsin side.

- Grassy Point and Kingsbury Bay cleanup, projected to jointly cost $14 million, is slated to begin in 2018. Material from Kingsbury Bay will help build wildlife habitat at Grassy Point.

As of 2016, ten contaminated river sites between Scanlon and the Twin Ports harbor still remained without sufficient funding for cleanup. The SLRA advocated at the Minnesota Legislature that year and the following year, ultimately securing $25.4 million in state bonding money to go toward matching the GLRI's $47.3 million for the cleanup of these sites. The availability of the federal funding made it an attractive and timely opportunity for the state to issue the bonding money. The state House, Senate, and Governor supported the request, and it was signed into law at the end of the 2017 session.

Also of note is the U.S. Steel project, which was expected to begin in 2018. The project entails cleaning up nearly two million cubic yards of sediment at a cost of $60-80 million. The U.S. Steel site is one of, if not the largest contaminated site on the Great Lakes — its cleanup, obviously significant.

The impressive and ongoing AOC cleanup effort has required participation and cooperation of countless people and organizations. But the truly remarkable part of this story is the community's stewardship, which sparked a massive, collective effort to heal our environment — hundreds of people claiming the problem as their own, committing to stay the course to restore our stretch of the St. Louis River. Community members of all walks gathered and assessed information in the early days following the AOC designation. They identified priorities, determined a path forward, and then forged ahead on that path toward what we've always known would be a long journey devoid of any instant gratification, personal incentive, and certainty. Weeks, months, years spent crafting complex strategies, sticking to a tireless plan, and step by step, we've moved toward a once-again flourishing, robust river, from bed to surface, bank to bank. ∎

William "Bill" Majewski worked for the City of Duluth Planning Department for 30 years. Upon retirement he was appointed to the WLSSD Board of Directors and served 12 years. In 2014 he was appointed to the Governors Coastal Council by Governor Dayton. He has been involved with the AOC since it was designated by the IJC in 1988, and has been active in the St. Louis River Alliance since it was formed in the early 1990s, currently serving as its chairperson.

CHAPTER

9

Clayton Jackson McGhie Memorial

BRINGING THE TRUTH TO LIGHT

by Heidi Bakk-Hansen

The story of how Clayton Jackson McGhie Memorial came to be must begin with the story of the lynching itself. In 1920, a mob of thousands of Duluthians tragically murdered three young black men, showing the world that our city was — sadly — no different than the dozens of other places in America where people acted out collective racial hatred with heinous public violence during that dreadful period between 1890 and 1930. Elias Clayton, Elmer Jackson and Isaac McGhie were three circus workers who, in a perversion of justice, were swept up in a nearly random fashion by police based on the dubious accusations of a young white couple from West Duluth, taken forcibly from the jail, and lynched from a lamppost on Second Avenue East and First Street.

The story might have ended there, stuck in shame and regret and fear. Instead, many people over the generations have passed down the truth of what happened that night, some who can be named, and others who cannot in the interests of space or anonymity. There was Michael Fedo, who wrote a book now titled *The Lynchings in Duluth*, and the first two small publishers who tried to bring that book to the public. There were several Duluth African-American community members who were interviewed by David V. Taylor in the 1970s, whose recollections of the lynching were recorded and preserved. There was Craig Grau and the First Lutheran Church, who marked and dedicated the three men's graves for the first time in 1991. And then there was the community, who refused to let the story continue on as just a shameful and inexplicable blot of deliberate forgetting in our city's history.

The first gathering of what would become the Clayton Jackson McGhie Memorial Committee was on June 15, 2000, when a front-page article about the lynchings came out in the Duluth *RipSaw*. In the article, I retold the story of what happened in 1920, made connections between this history and the present day, and named the accusers for the first time since the 1920s. This article coincidentally hit the streets at the same time as the first widely available publication of Fedo's book by the Minnesota Historical Society. A larger nationwide recognition stirred, too. America's history of racial terror that followed slavery had been largely neglected in the public consciousness. With the encouragement of Henry Banks, who was at that time a First Street business owner, a daylong vigil was held on the site of the lynching on its eightieth anniversary. Despite the persistent rain, people came to voice their personal grief, shock, and interest in something being done to bring the truth to light.

And so with the leadership of Banks and dozens of others who offered their support and labor that year, a grassroots committee began to meet regularly, its primary objective to determine how a memorial to the three men might come to be. Thirty people attended the first meeting. No person or organization had a reserved seat on the committee, but rather people belonged and lent their voice by showing up to meetings and serving on subcommittees around various issues and tasks.

It was generally agreed by committee members that the lynching was a community issue that needed addressing, that the event was historically significant, and that the memories of the three men had not been recognized with the appropriate gravity and permanence they deserved. Other primary missions of the committee were to ensure that the story of the lynching would be taught in Duluth public schools, and to create scholarships for Twin Ports youth.

A major obstacle facing us was the prevailing idea that negative history should be left behind. And while it might be discussed with academic remove, it should not be handled directly, with emotions laid bare, and it certainly didn't need a physical public place as a focal point. Meetings were held with Mayor Gary Doty in which he expressed his doubts, but he came to be persuaded and provided his leadership, as did many others who then came forward to offer their support, either by joining the committee or working within City Hall. Partnership with many organizations is important, and the willingness of city government to listen, support, and take part in the community's interest in racial justice is critical.

Although momentum slowly picked up, the committee, and the community at large, faced a decision, which we'd ultimately have to make collectively. Indeed, compelling reasons fortified two options — to pursue concrete commemoration of a shameful past, or not. Letting the shame live as it had since 1920 — abstractly, archived in stories and few scattered artifacts — was easier. Reflection could remain personal, optional. Building a memorial would take collective honesty, courage, and vulnerability.

We'd need to stride together on the messy walk toward atonement. Historical trauma, and the pain and discomfort that accompanies it, must be witnessed and acknowledged by the community as a whole in order for us to move forward together. Otherwise, we remain in a holding pattern of denial and avoidance.

It soon became clear, a memorial was a goal, but not an end — it'd be a place to start. At first, committee members were stuck on the idea of placing a plaque on the site where the lynching occurred. That corner was the location of a privately owned building, and its

The Clayton Jackson McGhie Memorial at Second Avenue East and First Street in Duluth.

owners were not receptive to anything being affixed there. Soon, we realized that the corner itself wasn't the only option available, and that there was an empty lot across the intersection that might hold more possibilities. The lot was owned by Lamar Advertising. The city agreed to heed the committee's call and pursue the lot, Lamar obliged, and creativity was granted a larger palette on which to work.

By 2001, a new subcommittee formed to work exclusively on creating a memorial plaza, in close partnership with the Duluth Public Arts Commission. Through this partnership, a request for

Heidi Bakk-Hansen

proposals went out nationwide. The December deadline that year was met with 17 proposals. The community at large was then invited to come and view models of the best designs and offer input. By February 25, 2002, Carla Stetson and Anthony Peyton Porter's proposal was selected. Their design was favored because of its intent and overall mission — engraved quotations stimulated reflection and discussion, and the gathering space offered a place for community reconciliation and healing.

Two committee members, Jill Caraway and Richard Dolezal,

Heidi Bakk-Hansen

Citizens gather at the Clayton Jackson McGhie Memorial in Duluth for the annual Day of Remembrance on June 15, 2016.

volunteered for the literally monumental task of coordinating the artists, contractors, committee, and commissions to make the chosen design a reality. For the rest of the committee, fundraising the projected $150,000 budget took center stage. Community events including concerts, a marathon reading of Fedo's book by local leaders, dinners and myriad other forms of money-making were devised in a time before the invention and widespread usage of online fundraising services. Hundreds of people contributed in one way or another, from community leaders to anonymous donors.

Meanwhile, writer Anthony Peyton Porter set to work getting input on selecting his quotations and writing the text that would accompany the three bronzes of Clayton, Jackson and McGhie, which were being created by artist Carla Stetson using three young area men as models. By September of 2002, the bronzes had been cast by American Bronze of Osceola, Wis. Artstone, of New Ulm, Minn. was selected to pour the walls, which they completed in the spring of 2003.

The unveiling of the memorial was on October 10, 2003 — a remarkable timeline from idea to completion, especially considering the sensitivity and controversial nature of its subject. There are cities all over America for whom this sort of memorial has proven an impossible task. It was attended by thousands of people from all over the country, including a great-grandson of one of the lynchers, who subsequently wrote a book about his experience. It has since served as it was intended to serve: a focal point for community gatherings that reflect on how history comes to impact our present, and how we as a community have a collective responsibility to address ongoing oppression, violence and hatred. The memorial is a place of hope. It stands today as the only one of its kind in the United States. It was truly raised by the nickels and dimes — and will — of the people.

The committee became a 501c3 nonprofit corporation, Clayton Jackson McGhie Memorial, Inc. Dozens of people have served on its board over the years, furthering its aims of education and racial reconciliation. A curriculum was written and offered to teachers. Scholarships are awarded each year to a deserving high school graduate, and in the past year, the board has begun to offer grants to youth in need of driver's licenses. In the summer of 2017, the board completed the first phase of the Duluth African-American Oral History Project, which will preserve the voices and stories of community members who have struggled and thrived here.

It has often been asked by locals and people visiting or studying this memorial from other places around the country who have a similar history: why Duluth? Why were we able to succeed when so many communities struggle for years — unsuccessfully — to get something as simple as a plaque placed to acknowledge similar incidents? This is, in some ways, a mystery and topic for scholars to discuss into the future. However, we would posit that it was a combination of ongoing, individual, persistent efforts over decades that finally reached a critical mass. A group of people were willing to break through public resistance and convince the community that this effort, although overdue, was not too late or impossible. We are a community that believes in progress, in movement toward a better future for all of us. ∎

Heidi Bakk-Hansen is a writer, researcher and teacher who moved to Duluth from Chicago in 1995. She was one of the co-founders of the Clayton Jackson McGhie Memorial and currently serves as the Clayton Jackson McGhie Board secretary.

CHAPTER

10

CHUM

PEOPLE OF FAITH WORKING TOGETHER

by Mary Schmitz

Since its grassroots inception, CHUM has housed and fed neighbors in the Central Hillside, and today, continues to chisel away at the barriers keeping people from reaching their full potential. CHUM began as a group of concerned Duluthians who pooled resources to help their neighbors, and has grown into a vast network of organizations partnering to dispel poverty and help people thrive. It's a collective approach that relies on community.

In the early 1970s, when the economic downturn began erasing good-paying manufacturing jobs and taking a toll on iron ore and shipping, people began to leave town. Many Duluthians who stayed found themselves working lower-income jobs and struggling to support their families. Requests for assistance grew steadily. Central Hillside Churches who recognized the magnitude of need banded together to address their inability to help everyone at their

Even children get in on raising food and funds for the CHUM Food Shelf. These exuberant third graders donated 642 pounds of food after they held a drive at their school, then helped unload the food, weigh it, and sort it.

doors. Discussions amongst church leaders ensued, and soon a group of Gloria Dei members responded in an effort known, in time, as Central Hillside United Ministries, John Hawley serving as the organization's first executive director.

In 1973 CHUM member congregations included:
    First Lutheran Church*
    First Presbyterian Church*
    First United Methodist Church*
    Gloria Dei Lutheran Church*
    Messiah Lutheran Church
    Peace United Church of Christ*
    Sacred Heart Catholic Church
    St. Anthony Catholic Church
    St. Peter's Catholic Church
    Trinity Lutheran Church*
    United Baptist Christian Church*
*Current member congregations

Clients, congregations, and community partners quickly adopted its acronym, CHUM.

Over time more and more Duluth churches from beyond the Central Hillside neighborhood became members of Central Hillside United Ministries and prompted the organization's name-change to Churches United in Ministry. Then, when Temple Israel joined, CHUM dropped its full name altogether, adopting the acronym as its official name. Today CHUM's membership includes 42 congregations as it continues to grow.

CHUM began to broaden its reach when use of food and shelter services continued to rise, revealing the need to address poverty in the community. The board of directors undertook the heavy task of identifying and advocating for societal changes that would prevent people from needing CHUM's emergency services.

Mission: CHUM is people of faith working together
to provide basic necessities, foster stable lives,
and advocate for a just and compassionate community.

In 2007, I sat in CHUM's administrative office awaiting my interview for the development director position. I realized while sitting there that I had worked for the same organization in the summers of 1978 and '79, in a program called Summer Center, which provided supervision, activities, and lunch for community children who otherwise had nowhere else to go while their parents worked during the day.

As I sat in that office, anticipating my interview, I realized how much I had enjoyed working with those children and all the teenaged staff we hired. We collaborated with local artists to foster creative experiences. We took the children to parks and even camping. The Duluth Schools' Summer Food Program collaborated with CHUM to provide lunches and snacks for the children. When I worked for the program, sites included First United Methodist Church, Grant (now Myers Wilkins) School, and St. Peter's Church (East Hillside). The program served up to 400 Duluth children each day.

I knew that between 1979 and 2007 CHUM, as an organization, had grown and changed. However, over the years, I hadn't paid close attention to what CHUM had become. But I did know that the organization was a good match for my personal mission. Two years prior to my interview, I had returned to Duluth after 5 ½ years of missionary work in a small Caribbean country where I worked with children and teenagers who were homeless.

I was happy to ultimately receive the position of development director at CHUM. Years later, I am proud of CHUM's work in the Duluth community.

COMMUNITY IMPACT

CHUM's programming has grown to include three divisions: stabilization services, distributive services, and congregational outreach and organizing.

STABILIZATION SERVICES

Kim Randolph heads up CHUM's stabilization services and recalls a time when one to ten people used the emergency shelter on any given night. That was 30 years ago, when Randolph began her career at CHUM. CHUM's shelter established at a time when relatively few people were living on the streets. Today, it is an essential service in Duluth, housing between 50 and 70 people per night. CHUM's shelter is the largest of two emergency shelters for adults and families in Duluth, the other being Safe Haven for women and children who have experienced domestic abuse.

The CHUM Center, which includes a shelter and a day center, are the more widely known and visible services CHUM offers. The CHUM Center's day program is known as the "drop-in center" for those who stay at the shelter at night, live in single room occupancy (SRO) rental units or board and lodging facilities, or need a safe place to socialize.

The CHUM Center is a place to find coffee and community, and consequently a doorway for people seeking assistance. By the time someone comes to CHUM, they often have already used up their welcome with family and friends, and are in severe need. No one really wants to come to CHUM, and it takes great courage to walk through the doors for the first time. However, once inside, a friendly and fair staff awaits, willing to help anyone through whatever issues necessary to move toward stabilization.

The CHUM Center provides basic self-care necessities, mail and phone services, and housing assistance from advocates who lead clients through the entire process of finding housing. The center provides lunches twice a week — paired with meals provided by Damiano's Soup Kitchen, Union Gospel Mission, community groups, and congregations, a community member in need can receive a hot meal every day.

In partnership with UMD's schools of pharmacy and medicine, Essentia Health, and Human Development Center, CHUM provides a health and wellness program, which includes health and dental care, education, and mental health services.

The street outreach program partners with the Duluth Police Department and St. Louis County Courts to provide a rehabilitative framework for repeat nuisance offenders to support their pursuit of housing and a better life path, thereby helping prevent overuse of the court system and jails.

Programs provided through the CHUM Center have changed over time as the needs of the community CHUM serves has grown and changed. Quickly and continuously adapting to meet the community's changing needs is one of CHUM's greatest hallmarks. Our services must adjust in order to stay viable as laws, rules, and regulations inevitably change. Only through its numerous vital partnerships and a reliance on working in concert with other organizations can CHUM provide and maintain its wide collection of services.

SHELTERING FAMILIES

In 1994, CHUM opened an emergency family shelter to answer the need for 24-hour shelter for families with children. CHUM's family housing advocate assisted families with enrolling their children in school, preschool, or daycare, while parents concentrated on finding income, affordable housing, and creating a plan to support their families. Depending on the family's barriers, this process could take three months or longer. Barriers to housing often include mental health issues, a felony record, poor rental or credit history, and general inability to stay housed.

Steve O'Neil Apartments

PERMANENT SUPPORTIVE HOUSING PLACING CHILDREN'S WELLBEING AT THE CENTER OF FAMILY LIFE

by Mary Lu Larsen

In 2011, CHUM, Center City Housing, and One Roof Community Housing (plus many other contributors) came together to address the increasing number of families experiencing homelessness who sought shelter at CHUM, and the critical need for more supportive housing options in Duluth. A building site was identified at the corner of Fourth Street and First Avenue West and construction began in December 2013.

The building was named the Steve O'Neil Apartments, after a much-loved St. Louis County Commissioner and longtime advocate for Duluth's homeless and poor. O'Neil, was widely respected and admired in the Duluth community. He passed away in July of 2013 after battling cancer.

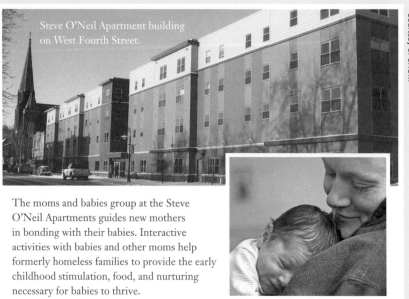

Steve O'Neil Apartment building on West Fourth Street.

Courtesy of CHUM

The moms and babies group at the Steve O'Neil Apartments guides new mothers in bonding with their babies. Interactive activities with babies and other moms help formerly homeless families to provide the early childhood stimulation, food, and nurturing necessary for babies to thrive.

Long-term homelessness is defined as being homeless for more than one year or four times within the last three years. Chronic homelessness has no timeframe and adds the burden of having a family member with a disabling condition. (HUD)

By 2008, the emergency family shelter was often exceeding its capacity, sending families with young children and newborn babies to stay at the congregate shelter with access limited to specific overnight hours. Gloria Dei Lutheran Church graciously stepped up, providing space and volunteers to house three families per night at the church in times of insufficient shelter space.

Ensuing discussions about a new emergency family shelter led CHUM leadership to partner with Center City Housing, One Roof Community Housing, the City of Duluth, the Housing and Redevelopment Authority, foundations, community businesses, corporations, faith-based communities and individual donors on an endeavor to address this need. Partners coalesced and built the Steve O'Neil Apartments, designed to meet the needs of families with children.

The Steve O'Neil Apartments opened in 2014 and are named for the late Steve O'Neil, St. Louis County Commissioner and longtime community leader and advocate for people experiencing homelessness and disenfranchisement. The new housing facility upholds a goal of ending the cycle of family homelessness by creating a culturally diverse community that keeps the wellbeing of children and their families at the center of community life.

DISTRIBUTIVE SERVICES

CHUM took over the Duluth Emergency Food Shelf program from the Duluth

STEVE O'NEIL APARTMENTS

Mary Schmitz of CHUM describes Mr. O'Neil:

Steve O'Neil had been a community organizer at CHUM and other agencies in Duluth prior to his election to the St. Louis County Board. Steve and his wife, Angie Miller, had started the Dorothy Day movement through the Loaves and Fishes community guesthouse for those in need of a welcoming home in which to shelter. Steve was not only an activist in the movement, but he and his family lived at Loaves and Fishes. Steve lived his passion that came through his faith. When it looked like the Hillside Apartments (the working name) were going to be a reality, he kicked into high gear to help raise funds in any way he could. Steve began using his contacts to encourage local folks to donate to the building project. He approached the DECC, which was hosting a Bob Dylan concert that summer, to allow CHUM volunteers to work the beer tent, where we ultimately earned $6,000 toward the project. When his friends

Continued on next page

STEVE O'NEIL
APARTMENTS
Continued from previous page

*planned a farewell party, he
insisted that all money raised
through donations and a
silent auction (which included
a large portrait of Steve),
would be contributed to the
building campaign. Everyone
knew that Steve O'Neil
full-heartedly stood behind
the project. When Steve
passed, he already knew there
was a plan afoot to name the
apartments for him. As the
humble servant Steve was, he
suggested naming them after
his favorite saints. Many
honorariums and memorials
for Steve helped us raise
significant dollars toward the
campaign. In the end, Steve's
family approved the naming
of the apartments for him.*

CHUM drew upon local
and national resources
to create a service
model for Steve O'Neil
Apartments that is now
uniquely at the forefront
of permanent supportive
housing practices. New
community partnerships
were established with area
social service agencies,
our public school system
and universities, health
care and dental providers,
mental health and

Food and Nutrition Council, a stand-alone
program run by a group of community
volunteers, in 1981.

And the following year, CHUM partnered
with Our Savior's Lutheran Church to open a
food shelf in West Duluth as more affordable
housing became available in the Lincoln
Park and Spirit Valley neighborhoods. By
1991, the CHUM food shelf was serving
9.8% of Duluth households, possible by the
support and contributions of the community
— congregations, volunteers, community
groups, and businesses.

CHUM's original food shelf was located
in several different places downtown, but is
currently housed in a small building across
the street from the CHUM Center. The
building's location better served drop-in-
center clients who requested food assistance,
and allowed CHUM to stockpile food
collected during the three annual food shelf
drives to distribute it effectively. This location
functions at top capacity today and serves up
to 70 food-insecure families twice a week.

In 2012 CHUM added a third food shelf
site in Lakeside after area churches reported
a need. Congregational volunteers fully
operate the site, serving 60 families every
year.

CHUM collects food and other donations
through various annual food drives, backpack
and school supplies drive, and individual
donations and drop-offs at the food shelf
sites. CHUM's needs list changes with time
and is updated online for anyone wanting to
conduct a drive or donate items directly.

CONGREGATIONAL OUTREACH AND ORGANIZING

Over 8,000 people attend one of CHUM's 42 member congregations in Duluth. They are a powerful force in advocating for public policies in the interest of the lowest-income members of our community. CHUM's organizing work is grounded in responding to those in need and loosening the bonds of injustice and oppression. While local and statewide partners change based on the current emphasis of CHUM's organizing efforts, CHUM's primary statewide advocacy partners are the Joint Religious Legislative Coalition (JRLC) and the Minnesota Coalition for the Homeless (MCH).

CHUM conducts outreach to foster congregational activities responding to the needs of the poor and disenfranchised, strengthen community by building relationships across the barriers that divide us, and bring about systemic changes that benefit the marginalized and dispossessed.

Because education is an important aspect of this effort, CHUM provides a four-hour course called "Expanding Horizons - A Local Poverty Awareness Program." This program gives community members the opportunity to learn about poverty, hunger, and homelessness in Duluth by meeting with organizations who work with people living these realities every day.

Engaging congregations and other community organizations through discussions, listening sessions, and presentations by local,

STEVE O'NEIL APARTMENTS

addiction recovery services, and new funding partners to build a support system for families with children who have experienced long-term or chronic homelessness. The Steve O'Neil Apartments opened in December of 2014, to provide permanent supportive housing for 44 families, as well as six emergency shelter units for families. Over a third of the families who moved into Steve O'Neil three years ago are still in residence today, which (for most) is significantly longer than they have ever lived anywhere before as adults.

Today, the Steve O'Neil Apartments provide a culturally supportive community that places the wellbeing of children at the center of family life. Family coaches help parents maintain stable housing, stay on track with goals and healthy behaviors, and build resilience in their own circumstances. Youth participate in after-school mentoring and tutoring activities and enrichment through summer camp

Continued on next page

STEVE O'NEIL
APARTMENTS
Continued from previous page

experiences and special outings. Young children benefit from a licensed therapeutic early childhood program that offers individualized attention, extra resources, and access to special education to help children overcome adversity. Families benefit from a support system that not only integrates community-based support services, but also organizes special activities that bring parents and children together to enjoy shared meals, and community gardening and harvesting projects. All programming is geared to build community within Steve O'Neil and help families overcome the effects of stress, trauma, and social isolation homelessness tends to cause. ∎

state and national leaders is integral to furthering the organization's mission.

Initiatives championed by CHUM have led to the development of new affordable housing, expanded health care options, increased public investment in stabilization services, and helped build safer neighborhoods in Lincoln Park, Central Hillside, East Hillside, Morgan Park, and West Duluth. Improvements in these neighborhoods percolate through our entire city.

At its core, CHUM feeds and houses neighbors in need. From there, CHUM maintains an evolving system of services to support our neighbors through their most difficult life challenges. We aim to lift up our citizens who are marginalized, homeless, and struggling to become self-sustaining and thriving. A broad and changing collection of barriers requires a broad and changing collective approach to breaking them down. CHUM is honored to serve as a connector, a bridge, between people, organizations, services, and access to a healthy life for everyone. ∎

Mary Lu Larsen is CHUM's Community Engagement Coordinator for the Steve O'Neil Apartments.

Mary Schmitz is CHUM's development director. Mary has always been drawn to helping people improve their lives and has worked and volunteered in a number of local nonprofits. Her past includes missionary work in St. Vincent and the Grenadines, working with children and teens who have experienced abandonment and abuse, and membership to the international Paralympic leadership team.

CHAPTER

11

Speak Your Peace: The Civility Project

PLEDGING TO ELEVATE COMMUNITY DIALOGUE

by Rob Karwath

Something wasn't right. In 2001, the Duluth Superior Area Community Foundation gathered a group of the Twin Ports' next generation of community leaders. It encouraged them to increase their levels of engagement on community issues.

The answer that came back was surprising — even shocking: No.

It wasn't that these young leaders didn't want to lead. Many, in fact, already were in leadership roles. But the problem identified by what was known as the Millennium Group was, in many ways, even more troubling. The quality of the public debate in the Twin Ports had sunk to such an uncivil level that even those who wanted to be involved didn't want to step up and do more. Some were even questioning their current levels of involvement.

Examples of public debates that devolved into nasty

fights included a proposal to bring the USS *Des Moines*, a mothballed war ship, to Duluth's lakefront as a tourist attraction, as well as City Hall budget issues and concerns about enrollment declines at the city's public schools.

Young leaders said they didn't mind the debates. But they were so turned off by the harsh rhetoric that they didn't want to get involved.

"That was not a sign of a healthy community," said Holly C. Sampson, president of the Community Foundation. "We realized that the long-term health of our community, from a social as well as an economic standpoint, was threatened by this perception of incivility, which was causing people not only to decide not to engage but, in some cases, to actually disengage. We had to do something about it."

The Community Foundation, one of the region's leading voices on social and community issues, was in a unique position to see this trend and to take action. It asked the Millennium Group, with leaders including local businessman Abbot Apter and City Council member (and future Duluth mayor) Don Ness to dig into the problem and find a solution.

Their finding was simultaneously simple and complex: Our community needed to focus on increasing the level of civility in public debate and everyday relationships if it wanted deeper involvement from the next generation of leaders.

Why was incivility such a problem? Our community behaviors were reflecting the often-uncomfortable change rippling across the nation and the world. The Twin Ports were responding in ways that turned off young people and others, leaving many feeling shunned. People weren't listening. They were pining for the days of old, when life was seemingly simpler. Change was scary. Northlanders were putting up walls and even working against change that they viewed as a threat — with gossip, a lack of respect, closed minds and an unwillingness to compromise.

Like most communities, division wasn't entirely new to Duluth and Superior. Issues of separation had always existed between the two cities and even between different neighborhoods and economic classes. Still, the diagnosis of incivility was difficult to hear. Yet the Millennium Group was unified in its voice: If the Twin Ports were to move ahead, they had to work for a greater understanding and practice of civility.

After drawing expertise from several sources, the Millennium Group developed Speak Your Peace: The Civility Project. It was a simple but powerful set of tools designed to address the simple but powerful problem of incivility. The tools could fit on the back of a wallet card — and did. The Speak Your Peace team developed a host of materials to promote the program. But to this day, the best known is the simple green wallet card that states the nine tools of civility.

The cards urged their holders to look inward and take action, pledging, "Today, I will." Then they listed the nine tools of Speak Your Peace that completed the pledge:

• Pay attention	• Not gossip	• Apologize
• Listen	• Show respect	• Give constructive criticism
• Be inclusive	• Be agreeable	• Take responsibility

If more Twin Ports residents used the simple tools of Speak Your Peace, the Millennium Group believed, relationships would grow stronger, ideas would bubble up, new opportunities would emerge — and the community would be better off. In addition, new people would feel more welcome and get involved, trusting that their voices would be heard, even if they didn't always prevail.

"Speak Your Peace was always about civic engagement," Sampson said, identifying one of the three foundational values of the Community Foundation, along with generosity and inclusiveness. "Communities with high levels of civic engagement are healthy and can find solutions or seize opportunities faster and better than others. They become destinations, and people invest in them — with their finances and with their lives."

The Community Foundation asked all six major units of local government — the city councils, the school districts and the county boards in Duluth and Superior — to adopt Speak Your Peace and begin modeling civil behavior. They did. The Duluth Public Schools went a step further and developed a middle school curriculum based

The nine tenets of Speak Your Peace: The Civility Project are represented on a poster that has been a familiar sight in public buildings, schools, churches and other places in the Twin Ports where people congregate. Since Speak Your Peace began in 2003, nearly 3,000 posters have been distributed in the Twin Ports, across the country and around the world.

One way that Speak Your Peace: The Civility Project continues to have impact in the Twin Ports is through regular training sessions. A popular program in 2017 and 2018 has focused on ways in which community members and participants in conversations can become better listeners, recognizing that "pay attention" and "listen" are the first two tenets of Speak Your Peace.

on Speak Your Peace to teach the next generation.

Speak Your Peace has been credited with bringing new ideas and people onto the political scene, perhaps best reflected by a new generation of candidates and elected leaders in both Duluth and Superior. It also helped Duluth overcome a municipal financial crisis in the mid-2000s.

The road to understanding and adoption wasn't always easy. After the launch of Speak Your Peace, some questioned whether ulterior motives — even political agendas — were behind the program. Others wondered whether it was truly needed. Still others felt insulted that some believed their hometown required a commitment to something as basic as civility.

But today, Speak Your Peace is one of the best-known public policy initiatives to come out of Duluth and Superior. Since its start in 2003, hundreds of programs and training sessions have been put on in the two communities and the surrounding region to teach and reinforce the benefits of Speak Your Peace. The little green cards, along with colorful Speak Your Peace posters, can be found throughout the Northland.

In addition, communities across the country and around the world have asked for training and to borrow the tools of Speak Your Peace, which are available online at dsaspeakyourpeace.org.

In 15 years, the program has been translated into Spanish, Hmong, Russian and Italian. It has helped communities as far away as California, Oregon, Texas and New York. It was named the winner of the first Minnesota Ethical Citizens Award in 2011. It has been developed into a high school curriculum by students and teachers at northern Wisconsin's Ashland High School. It is used and has been taught on dozens of college campuses in the United States and around the world.

These days, most in the Twin Ports react with familiarity and pride when they see the program's posters or cards, or hear about Speak Your Peace helping other places.

But whether far afield or close to home, Speak Your Peace still has work to do. The rapid pace of change is outstripping the ability of many individuals and communities to cope, let alone find new solutions. The fragmentation of media, especially online, has opened up many more options for news and information. But it also has established havens for consumers to receive only the news opinions that feel comfortable — and to associate only with those who speak and believe as they do. Polarization has increased in the halls of government, bringing civic wheels to a standstill on important local, state, and national issues.

"Speak Your Peace is needed as much, if not more, today than it was when we started it," Sampson said. "We're fortunate that Duluth and Superior realized it was necessary back then. We're fortunate that our community has developed a set of tools to help us and others find a brighter future through greater civility." ∎

Rob Karwath is president and CEO of North Coast Communications, a strategic communications firm based in Duluth, Minnesota. One of his clients is the Duluth Superior Area Community Foundation, where he provides media and communications counsel and also serves as the primary representative for introducing Speak Your Peace: The Civility Project to communities nationwide.

EVENTS

"The future doesn't belong to the fainthearted;
it belongs to the brave."

—Ronald Reagan, from his Address to the Nation, January 28, 1986

12

Homegrown Music Festival

DULUTH'S ANNUAL 200-BAND BLOWOUT

by Paul Lundgren

It was obvious from its inception the Homegrown Music Festival would become the flagship event for Duluth's music scene. There really wasn't any competition. That is to say it had been roughly two decades since any significant gathering of Duluth bands played more than one night together and called it a festival.

So, as silly as it might seem now, when Scott "Starfire" Lunt decided to book ten bands over two nights in the NorShor Theatre's mezzanine in 1999, it was considered utterly epic by the roughly 500 people who cared about such things back then.

It's not likely anyone thought in the beginning that Homegrown would grow to eventually span eight days, include 200 bands, have spinoff events in the Twin Cities and Iron Range, and require numerous committees and year-round planning. But there was an immediate sense

Andy Miller

Starfire at Clyde Iron Works, Homegrown 2012.

that Starfire had created something special — something local musicians and music lovers cherished.

It's not that Duluth was entirely devoid of culture prior to Homegrown, but as far as music was concerned the Bayfront Blues Festival took nearly all the headlines in the 1990s unless Mötley Crüe was booked at the Duluth Entertainment Convention Center. Most of the local bar bands played cover songs. A few folkies played coffee shop gigs. A handful of original bands played at the few bars that would have them — usually R.T. Quinlan's Saloon — and more often than not paired with a headliner from Minneapolis. The rest played basement shows and arranged performances at an old Northwestern

Bell telephone exchange building, dubbed "The RecylaBell." Prima donnas clearly need not apply.

A little Duluth band called Low had scored an indie record label deal and airtime on MTV in the 1990s, but probably fewer than half of one percent of Duluthians were aware of it. Duluth's music scene was deeply underground and wasn't coming up overnight.

Although Homegrown was immediately celebrated, embraced and sanctified by a circle of people yearning for a music festival authentic to Duluth, it didn't penetrate the consciousness of the average citizen or create any sense it might be sustainable until at least its tenth year. Before that it was merely a killer party for the bands and their friends, with the complete expectation the cops would eventually be called and everyone involved rounded up and sentenced to community service — sent to spend a few weeks scooping up monkey turds at the zoo before taking their little "music scene" back into the basement.

Indeed, the whole thing could have collapsed numerous times. Adversity lurks over every venture, after all. Homegrown has survived and thrived for twenty years because at every moment along the way someone cared enough to do the heavy lifting behind the scenes, and others took the risk of spilling art on a stage to see if anyone identified.

It started with Starfire, who organized the festival for six years — sometimes at a small profit, other times at a small loss, and always with hundreds of uncompensated hours of work. There were many helpers, but it was the founder who put his financial neck on the line and handled the brunt of the work in those early years.

Brothers Tim and Brad Nelson, along with a host of other friends, helped Starfire craft ideas for the festival and promote it. Prior to the first Homegrown, Brad Nelson started a newspaper with Cord Dada called the *Ripsaw*, which featured a heavy dose of Duluth music-scene news to educate the potential audience.

Dada took a sourcebook image of a chicken standing on top of a basket of eggs and used it to develop the first illustrated Homegrown logo. Twenty years later, Homegrown's mascot continues to be a chicken.

Doug Odlevek decorated the NorShor in the early years of Homegrown to give it a festival atmosphere. Dave Hoops started an

Aaron Reichow

Rachel Phoenix of Social Disaster, 2015 Main Club.

annual tradition by creating a special batch of beer called Homegrown Hempen Ale. Mark Lindquist organized the festival schedule a few times as the list of bands started getting longer. When Starfire was traveling with Low as nanny for Alan and Mimi Sparhawk's daughter Hollis, Tim Anderson stepped up to coordinate Homegrown.

In 2005 the number of bands reached 90. Starfire had taken it as far as he could. Tim and Brad Nelson became the new owners, working with *Ripsaw* staff — primarily Brandy Hoffman — to make it all happen. But it was just too much. How does a for-profit festival pay 90 bands, hire sound engineers and a staff to coordinate all the shows, and then charge just $15 for weekend passes?

It was this moment in time when Homegrown was at its weakest. Though in seven years it had grown from 10 bands to 90, and was drawing more and more of an audience, the logistics and public relations were becoming unmanageable. It could have all slipped away.

Don Ness was the guy who stepped in next, organizing a handful of committees to manage Homegrown as a nonprofit, then taking on the roll of festival director. He hit the ground running, expanding Homegrown from a four-day to an eight-day event with more than 100 bands. He added poetry, videos and visual arts to the mix.

New challenges emerged: The *Ripsaw* folded, the NorShor temporarily closed, the Twin Ports Music and Arts Collective collapsed. Ness soldiered on. Homegrown developed an annual magazine-style festival program called the *Field Guide* for promotion. New websites and 'zines filled the *Ripsaw* void. New venues opened. Digital photography exploded and photos from Homegrown helped show off the atmosphere of the festival.

Ness moved on to become mayor of Duluth, and Paul Connelly was tapped to take over Homegrown in 2007. It was another critical moment. Would the new nonprofit thrive with a musician at the helm instead of a politician?

The festival was still growing in terms of the number of bands eager for a slot to play, but the basic format was largely established. With the help of a hardworking committee — particularly Dave Mehling in a pinch — Connolly kept Homegrown prospering.

When Shana David-Massett took over before the 2010 Homegrown, she had only lived in Duluth about a year. She barely managed to get accepted for a performance slot in the previous Homegrown. Then suddenly she was in charge of it.

It was somewhere in the smooth transition from Connolly to David-Massett when people close to the festival became confident it could go on for another decade or more. And it was also at this time when the general public — not just barflies and hardcore music fans — started to recognize the festival by name.

Growth and stability followed when Walter Raschick took over as festival director. If there's a name to rival Starfire in the annals of Homegrown history it would be "Walt Dizzo." Raschick started volunteering for Homegrown in 2007, became a steering committee member in 2009, and served as festival director from 2012 to 2016.

Melissa La Tour took over from there. She'd been helping the festival along from the very beginning in one way or another. Close at her side are a handful of board members, a dozen steering committee members, various directors and coordinators, and hundreds of volunteers.

Though Homegrown's financial and organizational struggles always seem difficult to manage, as time passes it's surprising how easily it seems those challenges are transcended. But the balance remains tenuous. What will always be needed to keep Homegrown going is legions of dedicated people volunteering to do the little things, all led by at least one heavy lifter inspired to properly shepherd them.

There's more to it than that, though. All the nerdy organizational stuff would never have amounted to much if it wasn't for the musicians, who don't just show up on time and go through the motions, but always seem to put extra energy into their Homegrown shows because they know it's Duluth's biggest week for music. Many of them understand where the music scene came from and how it got here. They know Homegrown is more about camaraderie than music, but the music makes it all possible. And they know what they have is fragile.

It's also unique. Other communities don't have it. There are much bigger music festivals than Homegrown and a lot of cities with events that showcase exclusively local talent. But there is no other community in the world where 200 bands with connections to the same community come together to share their talents.

Brad Nelson, who has drummed for various bands during Homegrown's first twenty years, in addition to his aforementioned roles co-founding the *Ripsaw* and organizing the festival, may have stated it best in a Homegrown retrospective years ago:

"Homegrown is the axle the music scene revolves around. It pulls it all together. I can't imagine what the Duluth music scene would be like without it." ∎

Paul Lundgren started writing about Homegrown as editor of the Ripsaw *newspaper at the turn of the millennium and never stopped. He has directed the content of every edition of the* Homegrown Field Guide *and served on the festival's steering committee from 2006 to 2010. His other chief fixation in life is a website called* Perfect Duluth Day.

13

Bentleyville

THE LIGHTS FANTASTIC

by Amy Norris

In 2001 Nathan Bentley decorated his Esko home in lights — lots of lights — for the Christmas season. The next year he added more lights; his home soon became known as the "house-with-all-the-lights-in-Esko."

In 2003, Nathan changed his light display from a "drive-by" to a "walk-through." When Santa Claus started visiting on the weekends, a friend sarcastically started calling the display "Bentleyville," poking fun at Nathan's over-the-top venture. The name caught on with visitors, and "Bentleyville Tour of Lights" was born.

During the summer of 2004, Nathan and his family moved from Esko to rural Cloquet to a larger home for their four children. With the new name of "Bentleyville" came a whole new vision for Nathan. To entice people to drive out into the country to see the light display, it had to be larger and grander yet. So larger and grander

Bentleyville 2017 illuminates the waterfront as a ship exits the harbor under the Aerial Lift Bridge.

it became — a 78-by-24-foot entrance castle made of 45,000 lights now greeted visitors, and over 500 illuminated snowflakes hung from trees overlooking dozens of light displays. Pretty soon, fire pits welcomed marshmallow roasting, Santa became a permanent fixture, and area school groups and community musicians performed live at Bentleyville.

Then came the "Cookie House;" paved walking paths; a popcorn stop; and a food and toy drive for the Salvation Army.

As Bentleyville and its popularity grew quickly, so did traffic and parking problems on the dead-end country dirt road. Neighbors grew concerned, and something had to be done about the congestion. After just two years at the new location and an estimated 35,000 visitors, Nathan decided the only way to solve the parking issue was to use

Photo by Dennis O'Hara/Northern Images Photography

nearby horse fields owned by area neighbors for parking. Visitors would be bussed in by nine hired 72-passenger school busses to run between two parking fields and the Bentleyville entrance.

In 2008, after five years of hosting Bentleyville at his residence and transporting over 72,000 people by school bus, Nathan thought it was a good time to take a year off and re-think how everything was working.

In the fall of that year off, I came into the story. I was a public information coordinator for the City of Duluth, and I was honored to call Nathan, inviting him to a meeting with Mayor Don Ness to discuss the possibility of moving Bentleyville Tour of Lights to Bayfront Festival Park in Duluth.

After meeting, Nathan thought Bayfront would be a good fit for

Bentleyville and accepted a one-year trial run.

Planning began immediately for the large undertaking of moving Bentleyville to a venue four times the size of the Bentley residence. Nathan selected a board of directors, established a nonprofit organization, and asked his original Bentleyville team of 25 people to help organize and plan for a Christmas light show at Bayfront in need of more than 600 volunteers and taking at least 10 weeks to set up.

As excitement of Bentleyville at Bayfront grew, so did support from Duluth business leaders, enthused by the prospect of drawing people downtown in the cold winter months.

On Friday, November 27, 2009, Bentleyville Tour of Lights turned on its millions of lights to thousands of onlookers for the first time at Bayfront Park in downtown Duluth. Over 150,000 people visited Bentleyville that first year.

Bentleyville continues its tradition of expansion in its Bayfront home. A 128-foot-tall animated tree stands as its iconic centerpiece, alone boasting 150,000 LED lights! The Cookie House and marshmallow-roasting fire remain as fixtures, and awe-inspiring walk-through light tunnels are crowd favorites. In 2016, Santa Claus & Mrs. Claus skydived into Bentleyville on opening night. Attendance surpassed 292,00 people that season.

People of all ages await the anticipated unveiling of new displays and a fresh new look each year; for the Duluth community, and for countless families from near to far, Bentleyville has become a holiday must. 2018 marks the 15th season of Bentleyville Tour of Lights. ∎

Native Duluthian Amy Norris has been involved in community and state activities for over 30 years. Several highlights of her professional career include hosting an ISD 709 television program on PBS, lobbying for the final $14 million to complete the Lake Superior Aquarium, serving as executive director of Kids Voting Minnesota, and teaching American Sign Language at UMD for over 20 years. The daughter of deaf parents, Amy has advocated for the rights of people with disabilities throughout her lifetime and has volunteered in numerous civic organizations. Her love for Duluth, family, and friends has kept her happily living here. Her infectious smile and warm personality brings happiness to people who meet and know her.

CHAPTER

14

Tall Ships Duluth

THE GREATEST SPECTACLE ON LAKE SUPERIOR

by Terry Mattson

> *"Dream big.*
> *To accomplish great things*
> *we must not only act, but also dream;*
> *not only plan, but also believe."*
>
> —Anatole France

The sights and sounds of majestic tall ships entering the Duluth harbor — sails rippling, ropes whizzing, cannons booming — are unforgettable. History comes alive when tall ships appear on the Lake Superior horizon and sail in toward Duluth's harbor to thousands of onlookers waiting on the waterfront.

Tall Ships Duluth, the "Greatest Spectacle on Lake Superior," draws about 250,000 fans (nearly three times Duluth's population) who contribute roughly $15 million to the local economy, and creates a tidal wave of public

Niagara, news helicopter overhead; crowd favorite, comes every festival year. (2010)

Paul L. Hayden

interest. Weekend attendance rivals that of the Minnesota State Fair.

As president and CEO of Visit Duluth, the city's convention and visitor's bureau, from 1990 to 2013, I had the honor of leading tourism branding and sales during a period of unprecedented growth. I also had the pleasure of creating and producing Tall Ships Duluth — and now, the pleasure of telling the story of how Duluth began orchestrating multi-ship visits and drawing visitors from every U.S. state and Canadian province.

The metrics of the event are impressive and have real-life implications for Duluth's businesses, jobs, and families.

HISTORY

In the late 1800s there were approximately 2,000 tall ships, traditional large sailing ships, on the Great lakes. The Twin Ports probably saw days with 65 sails in port. Developments in marine engineering and technology systematically replaced tall ships with modernized vessels. Today, tall ships are a novelty.

Sorlandet nears the DECC area. (2013)

In 1976 Norway's tall ship *Christian Radich* made an appearance to cheering crowds in Duluth as part of America's Bi-Centennial. Later, in 1985, the city brought in a small schooner named the *T.S. Merkur*. In 1986, Duluth's port nearly became home to the 127-foot, three-masted schooner *Victory Chimes*, but plans fizzled.

As a staff member of the convention and visitor's bureau since 1985, I gained experience promoting a handful of single-ship events before committing Visit Duluth to three vessels, simultaneously, in 2008. Thus began Tall Ships Duluth.

Tall ships are "rockstars of the sea," navigating the globe for hire — we needed to make Duluth a port of call on their "concert tour." That meant collaboration with other Great Lakes and world ports, assuming financial responsibility, and selling thousands of admission tickets. Since no one else on Lake Superior had ever done this before, and Duluth is the world's farthest inland port, it would be a massive challenge.

VISION

The vision did not initially have universal buy-in. There were powerful skeptics. Some thought it was a ridiculous notion with too much risk. Even some hoteliers could not envision the benefits to come. Visit Duluth's board chairs during that time, Kristi Schmidt, Tony Bronson, and Karen Pionk, in succession, deserve credit for their tenacity in backing the strategy.

The American Sail Training Association, now known as Tall Ships America, assisted generously in bringing tall ships to Duluth. Tall Ships America's mission "is to encourage character building through sail training, promote sail training to the North American public, and support education under sail" (*Tall Ships America*, n.d.). Patricia Lock and Bert Rogers of Tall Ships America™ played a critical role in building the fleets we welcomed. While multi-ship visits took place in other parts of the world, bringing the ships to Lake Superior was unchartered territory.

In 2008, Visit Duluth brought in the *Pride of Baltimore II*, U.S. Brig *Niagara* and the *Madeline*. As the ships neared port, automobile traffic was backed up as far as one could see south from the Fifth Avenue West overpass on I-35. We attracted 125,000 people in three days along with immeasurable publicity. It was clear — the tall ships had piqued widespread interest.

"About halfway through Duluth's 2008 tall ships festival that brought three sailing vessels to the city, Visit Duluth President Terry Mattson said 'I NEED MORE SHIPS.'"

—Duluth News Tribune, 2008

While the first multi-ship visit was indeed successful, it's Tall Ships Duluth 2010 that doubled attendance and will go down in history as a milestone event. For a large portion of our visitors, the 2010 event was their first introduction to the region. Visit Duluth partnered with the University of Minnesota-Duluth to put on a nine-ship extravaganza with an unparalleled entertainment atmosphere. The university brought an abundance of art and culture to the scene. Eight thousand people turned out for "Pirates of Penzzance" on the Lois M. Paulucci main stage at Bayfront Festival Park, thanks to UMD's Chancellor Kathryn Martin, and School of Fine Arts Dean Jack Bowman.

The collaborative enthusiasm from an exhaustive list of supporters made it all happen. Stakeholders included the City of Duluth, local business sponsors, U.S. Coast Guard, MNDOT, Duluth Seaway Port Authority, Duluth Playhouse, Draw Events, Grandma's Restaurant Corporation, the DECC, Great Lakes Aquarium, Duluth Police Department, On the Limit, and many more that worked together for two years on planning, logistics, and promotion.

More than 300 volunteers cannot be thanked enough.

Duluth Rotary Club 25 was our first major sponsor; its volunteers sold water to patrons at bargain prices during sweltering temperatures. The Duluth Superior Eco Rotary Club's volunteers helped thousands of guests find their way each day.

With the help of WLSSD and Hartel's/DBJ Disposal, guests knew where to recycle items throughout the venue, and the event smashed records for the amount of recyclables collected at a single event in Duluth.

The Visit Duluth staff worked tirelessly, bringing to the event's planning and production a local, personal commitment to Duluth. And Duluth's citizens welcomed a record number of visitors. The collective effort — visionaries, supporters, sponsors, volunteers, staff, ticket-buyers, ship crewmembers — made Tall Ships Duluth 2010 the biggest tourism week in Duluth's history.

In 2011, we contracted with three tall ships in a pilot run for day sails, rides aboard the vessels. We ultimately incorporated day sails into another full-blown ten-ship festival in 2013.

The summer of 2013 would be my last as president/CEO of Visit Duluth before embarking on new career adventures. Tall Ships Duluth 2013 proved successful in spite of inclement weather. It turns out tall ships fans are a hearty bunch.

Visit Duluth later handed off the tall ships torch to Draw Events, a local event company whose owner, Craig Samborski, was previously contracted for Tall Ships Duluth event logistics. Craig and his team brought the World's Largest Rubber Duck to Duluth for Tall Ships 2016.

The insights and leadership of HTK Marketing (now Hailey Sault) — Mike Seyfer, Marsha Hystead, and founder, Howard Klatzky — deserves recognition for its work in building not only this event, but Duluth tourism overall. Visit Duluth's partnership with Lake Superior Magazine — Cindy and Paul Hayden — and their passion for the region went above and beyond expectations. Explore Minnesota, the state's tourism agency, and its director, John Edman, were catalysts for promoting the Duluth event broadly.

Tall Ships Duluth grew to be the single largest event in northern Minnesota history. And with roughly a million dollars on the line in producing it, it's riskier than most events, too. But the event's success proves its risks worthwhile. And Duluth needs risk-takers; a great place doesn't become greater without them. Each Tall Ships Duluth event, in addition to generating tax revenue, achieved its break-even financial goal and added money to the coffers for future events.

Tall Ships Duluth has given locals and visitors the opportunity to catch a glimpse of, or set foot aboard, some of the most heralded ships of yore — and to do so in a place largely defined by its waters and celebrated history of shipping.

It's my hope that everyone who has contributed to bringing tall ships to Duluth feels proud to have played a role. Tony Bronson said it best: "The event showcases Duluth at its finest, and the positive ripple effects of those grand ships reach far beyond these few days." ∎

Terry Mattson enjoyed a 28-year career at Visit Duluth leading destination marketing efforts before becoming president & CEO at Visit Saint Paul and the RiverCentre in 2014. He was also the creator and former executive producer of Tall Ships Duluth. While in the Twin Cities, Mattson has held roles in other large events, such as the Super Bowl, Red Bull Crashed Ice, PGA Ryder Cup, and the NCAA Frozen Four.

ECONOMIC DEVELOPMENT

"Exploration is the engine that drives innovation.
Innovation drives economic growth.
So let's all go exploring."

—Edith Widder

CHAPTER

15

Bluestone

CREATING DULUTH'S OWN "DINKYTOWN"

by Keith Hamre

By the early 2000s, Duluth had become a higher education destination. Duluth's three main college institutions had expanded significantly since the early '90s, a wave of robust investment and growth that ultimately spanned 20 years. Systematic investment and growth continues today.

The institutions themselves, along with their respective growth, work in concert for a number of reasons, but prominent are the three schools' distinctive roles. Lake Superior College is a community and technical college, and in addition to its two-year pre-baccalaureate degree program, collaborates with local and regional businesses to specialize numerous certificate and degree programs to meet current workforce needs. The College of Saint Scholastica (CSS) is an independent private college offering undergraduate and graduate liberal arts programs rooted in Catholic Benedictine values. The University of Minnesota

UMD Expansion

A GREAT UNIVERSITY ON A GREAT LAKE

The University of Minnesota Duluth (UMD) underwent a 15-year expansion under the leadership of its first woman chancellor, Kathryn A. Martin, who arrived at UMD in 1995 with architectural expertise, a successful fundraising background, and at the start of a nationwide era of college campus upgrades.

Higher education prospered during Martin's tenure, thanks in part to the baby-boom echo generation and expansion of academic resources. UMD's enrollment grew from 7,500 in 1996 to 11,300 in 2009, prompting a shift from the institution's roots in teacher training to a stronger focus on STEM (Science, Technology, Engineering and Mathematics) fields and business. Even though the legislature's contribution toward the cost of education had dwindled substantially by the '90s, UMD continued to thrive, buoyed by tuition from an expanded student body, the Northeastern Minnesota legislative delegation support for construction, and increased private philanthropic support. Development efforts became big business in the public higher education sector nationally, following a traditionally private-school model of heavy reliance on private support. Martin expanded outreach in light of this trend, engaging alumni to broaden UMD's support base.

Courtesy of UMD

Aerial view of UMD's campus (2013).

Duluth (UMD) is a major regional university offering 93 undergraduate programs and 20 graduate programs.

Each school fills a niche in the community and region, offering very different programs and each thriving in its own way. The complementary nature of the three campuses has fortified the higher education sector in Duluth, and the community reaps a dynamic set of benefits, and in turn, a dynamic set of challenges.

Duluth's growing college student population has challenged the community to evolve to meet the students' needs. One major need students have made clear: housing with walkable access to campus and amenities.

Duluth's long, narrow layout and its steep, rocky ledges create geographical separation of neighborhoods and commercial districts. Duluth's college campuses stand, in many ways, encapsulated, isolated from other non-residential parts of the city. And in the early 2000s, challenges in the neighborhoods surrounding CSS and UMD converged in a substantial strain that could no longer be managed piece by piece as the student population continued to grow.

Students aimed to live close to campus, which prompted the conversion of numerous single-family homes in those near-campus neighborhoods to student rental houses. In time, poor property upkeep began to degrade the beauty of the neighborhoods; streets became overcrowded, eliminating reliable on-street parking for longtime residents;

UMD EXPANSION

Behind Martin stood a leadership team, whose members are now retired with more than 125 combined years of service. This core group, who welcomed Martin to campus and, with her, effectively reinvented UMD's physical image, included UMD alumnus Greg Fox, vice chancellor for finance and operations; Bruce Gildseth, vice chancellor for academic support and student life; Vince Magnuson, vice chancellor for academic administration; and UMD alumnae Diane Skomars, director of development and university relations. This veteran UMD team tirelessly pushed Martin's aggressive building agenda forward. Fox expertly navigated the bureaucracy of the University of Minnesota system and capitalized on long-term relationships with members of the Northeastern Minnesota legislative delegation. Magnuson advocated for and led the development of several new academic initiatives and worked with the collegiate

Continued on next page

UMD EXPANSION
Continued from previous page

unit leaders to hire faculty
and staff to support them.
Gildseth bolstered the
student life experience for
the growing student body,
from the new multicultural
center to renovations in
Kirby Student Center.
Skomars built a strong
development team and
traveled extensively with
the chancellor, garnering
a substantial increase in
private donations needed
to realize Martin's vision.

These factors — a
talented university
leadership team, growing
student body, legislative
and communtiy support,
and a strong philanthropic
base — spurred a
$167-million campus-
wide construction boom,
including renovation and
new buildings, which
effectively changed the
campus footprint.

• Building UMD's third
  library became Martin's
  highest priority. In 1996,
  the Minnesota State
  Legislature funded its
  planning, and ground
  was broken two years
  later. The $26-million
  library was dedicated
  in 2000. Designed by

City planning map showing the Woodland Middle School
site prior to Bluestone's construction.

and college nightlife disrupted families. The
change took a toll on neighborhoods, and
tense discussions ensued between residents
about what it meant to be good neighbors.

In 2008, the "Higher Education Small
Area Plan," the product of a student
housing needs study by the city's planning
department, specified a need for mixed-use
development — development that includes
a well-connected mixture of uses; in this
case, commercial/retail, institutional, and
housing — in either the Kenwood or Mount
Royal neighborhood, a model similar to
Minneapolis' "Dinkytown." Both Kenwood

Courtesy of City of Duluth

UMD EXPANSION

Duluth's Stanius Johnson Architects as the most technologically advanced library in Minnesota, the 167,000-square-foot space includes a two-story copper dome rotunda with panoramic views. In 2013, the building was renamed the Kathryn A. Martin Library.

• The $9.2-million Weber Music Hall, designed by Cesar Pelli, world-famed architect, opened in 2002. The hall was named in honor of alumni Mary Ann and Ron Weber, who made major gifts toward the design and completion of the building, which creates the intimate feel of a small concert hall under a striking 85-foot-tall copper dome and a dramatic skylight. The Weber Music Hall completed the arts triangle in the UMD Ordean Court, accompanying the Tweed Museum of Art and the Marshall Performing Arts Center.

• In 2004, Kirby Student Center underwent

Continued on next page

and Mount Royal have commercial districts and are within close proximity to the two main college campuses. The plan, completed with intensive community input, presented an opportunity to solve neighborhood problems that had resulted from the influx of student rental properties.

Two other planning processes, the City of Duluth's comprehensive planning process and the Duluth School District's long-range facilities planning process, revealed the same favored notion: mixed-use development in Kenwood or Mount Royal. Also in those planning processes, the former Woodland

UMD EXPANSION
Continued from previous page

major renovation, including the addition of a multicultural center with student offices and lounge, and a three-story plaza, including an enlarged bookstore, new food court, expanded DTA bus hub, childcare center, administrative offices, and coffee shop.

- The $12.4-million addition to the UMD Sports and Health Center opened in 2006, making the facility the largest and most comprehensive athletic and recreational sports center in Northern Minnesota. Funded partially by student fees, the two-story fitness center overlooks Malosky/Griggs and houses space for recreational fitness programs and the athletic department's team training.

- In 2007, the $15.2-million renovation of the UMD Life Science Building was completed. The renovated space houses the College

Businesses at Bluestone seen from above Summit Street turnabout, looking westward toward Woodland Avenue.

Middle School site, which had served the Duluth School District from 1958 to 2009 and now stood in growing disrepair, emerged as an opportune place for redevelopment.

The community had worked to articulate a major need and identify a potential site to meet the need. The City of Duluth and the Duluth School District thereby partnered to seek a developer willing to create a mixed-use development suitable for the Woodland site and geared toward meeting student housing needs. Mark Lambert of Summit Management, who had previously developed Campus Park and Boulder Ridge

Boulevard Real Estate Photography

UMD's Malosky Stadium and Griggs Field are visible in the background.

student housing developments in Duluth, stepped forward, ready to take on the challenge. He ended up purchasing the old Woodland Middle School property in 2011. Mark envisioned remaking the place into a destination mixed-use development that the community could be proud of. It was an unproven design in Duluth at that time, but Mark's concept of a well-designed, blended commercial and residential complex built around a theme resonated with the community.

Soon after purchasing the property, Mark began the public process necessary

UMD EXPANSION

of Pharmacy and the Department of Biology. Paddock Laboratories, led by Duluth native and President Bruce Paddock, donated $2 million to the University of Minnesota College of Pharmacy toward the project.

- The $33-million James I. Swenson Science Building, designed by Carol Ross Barney, acclaimed Chicago architect, was completed in the winter of 2005. The construction was made possible by the largest single gift ever given to UMD. James I. Swenson, a 1959 graduate of UMD, and the Swenson Family Foundation donated $10 million to UMD, which included $7.5 million toward the building and $2.5 million toward science student scholarships and undergraduate chemistry research programs.

- The $23-million Labovitz School of Business and Economics, designed by Ralph E.

Continued on next page

UMD EXPANSION
Continued from previous page

Johnson, renowned Chicago architect, opened in the summer of 2008. The school is named for Duluth native and UMD alumnus Joel Labovitz and his wife, Sharon, who made a gift of $4.5 million. The gift was the largest ever for the school and the second largest for UMD. Their generosity helped secure legislative support for the remaining cost of the building, which became the first LEED (Leadership in Energy and Environmental Design) certified facility in the University system. Located on the northwestern corner of the campus, the facilities provide a new gateway to campus and showcase UMD's commitment to sustainability .

• In 2008, a $6.5-million overhaul of Malosky Stadium included concessions, UMD stores, club space, press box, and more seating. The James S. Malosky Stadium is named after the legendary Jim Malosky, who led the

Aerial view of the Bluestone development looking northward. Bluestone Lofts appear in the upper right.

to fulfill the vision. Reaching the desired end would require property rezoning and the development of a Tax Increment Financing (TIF) district. TIF is a financing tool whereby the city pledges to use the newly generated property taxes to pay for, or finance, public infrastructure like roads, water, sewer and site preparation — in this case, soil correction and rock removal. Those who attended Woodland Middle School (myself included) know about "The Rock." A fair amount of that aptly named blue Gabbro ledge was ultimately removed from the site to make way for utility

Boulevard Real Estate Photography

UMD EXPANSION

Bulldogs for 40 years and was the winningest coach in NCAA Division II football history at the time.

• The $15-million Swenson Civil Engineering Building, designed by Carol Ross Barney, opened in 2010. Located on the northeast corner of the campus, the teaching/training center houses the Bachelor of Science degree program in civil engineering, which admitted its first students in 2008 and graduated its first class in 2012. UMD benefactor and 1959 graduate, James I. Swenson of the Swenson Family Foundation donated $3 million to support the building's construction.

• The Bagley Classroom opened in 2010 and is in the Bagley Nature Area adjacent to campus. Designed by David Salmela, internationally noted Duluth architect, the Bagley Classroom is a zero-energy and nearly zero-waste building and received LEED platinum status.

Continued on next page

infrastructure for the new development. And in honor of the rock upon which it would sit, the new development became known as Bluestone.

The hoped reuse of the former school building eventually proved financially infeasible when concepts continually fell through — college classrooms, learning center, fitness center, among others — and the building was razed to enable construction of modern facilities. Later in the process, CSS proposed and funded building a new learning center at Bluestone, bringing in an educational component to round out the

UMD EXPANSION
Continued from previous page

- Full renovation of many existing buildings also occurred during Martin's tenure. In every case, the classrooms were modernized, public spaces brightened, asbestos removed, and air conditioning added.

UMD's construction boom supported Duluth's building trades and bolstered UMD's public relations. The corresponding growth in academic programs — namely STEM and business — attracted new students, including many from the Twin Cities. The uptick in enrollment ushered in some new challenges, indeed — operational issues on campus and strain on neighborhoods bearing the challenges of rapid growth. In time though, the community has answered these challenges with innovation and improvement. And the campus has shed its uninviting physical image for a dynamic, modernized environment that better matches UMD's spirit. ∎

development's offerings.

Today, Bluestone is dynamic, modern, and meets the students' and community's needs the developer and city originally set out to meet. Primarily inhabited by UMD and CSS students, the residential buildings of Bluestone also house professionals and empty-nesters. Retail, services, and restaurants comprise four commercial buildings, welcoming the whole community to Bluestone.

Campus-area neighborhoods have seen alleviation from issues associated with a high density of student rental properties. The Bluestone redevelopment has been transformational for the community and has spurred new interest in functional multi-family housing and mixed-use development, including other projects like Endi, Kenwood Village, and District Flats at Miller Hill. These projects in other areas of the city similarly take pressure off of densely populated neighborhoods, restore single-family housing in residential spaces, and meet the growing demand for that style of housing. ∎

Keith Hamre has been with the City of Duluth since 1997. He has served as the manager of the city's community development and housing and now serves as the director of planning and construction services. He managed the development agreement and rezoning for the Bluestone project.

CHAPTER

16

Duluth Heritage Sports Center

IT'S MUCH MORE THAN HOCKEY

by Richard Loraas
and contributing authors
Patrick Francisco and Jerry DeMeo

The story of the Duluth Heritage Sports Center follows a fascinating journey resulting in quite a miracle. Hundreds of Duluthians of all stripes coalesced around a vision to create a value-centered community facility that will serve our children and families for generations to come. With no paid staff and all volunteers, this great effort persevered through numerous setbacks, crises, and the worst recession since the 1930s — a shining example of what can happen when people align toward a common vision and rely on their own ingenuity.

THE BEGINNING

In 2004, a tragic fire reduced the Ray Peterson ice arena to ashes at Wheeler Field. By 2005, the City of Duluth and Duluth Amateur Hockey Association (DAHA) agreed it was important to construct a replacement arena on the original site. The City pledged $2.3 million in insurance proceeds if DAHA raised $1.8 million in private contributions. The new arena, like the former one, would be owned by the city and operated by DAHA. A design contract emerged with DSGW architects of Duluth, and the process to build a new arena began.

DAHA organized a group to help with fundraising; members included Clarke Coole, John Scott, Patrick Francisco, Nancy Nilsen, Terry Scott, Joe McCulloch, and others.

The initial design was a larger arena with a retro feel, similar to the Eveleth Hippodrome, including artificial ice and a substantial display interpreting Duluth's rich hockey history.

OOPS

While the committee organized to raise private funds, a thousand-pound gorilla entered the scene. The City of Duluth had entered a contest to become a site for the Kroc Foundation community center through the Salvation Army. The application listed Wheeler Field as the proposed location for this very large and comprehensive center. The contest set our arena project on hold while the Kroc Center design took shape. Then after several months spent trying to make both projects work together, the parameters of the Salvation Army requirements eliminated possible benefits for our project. We decided to seek an alternative site and allow the Kroc Center proposal to proceed without added complication.

> "No matter the adversity or difficult economic conditions faced, the honorable people behind the goals of the Duluth Heritage Sports Center never gave up."
>
> —Craig Fellman, President Jamar Company

OPPORTUNITY KNOCKS – A NEW DIRECTION

A search ensued for an alternative site – Wade Stadium, Duluth's west hillside, others. Mayor Bergson suggested that we consider Fourth Avenue West and Second Street, which included a possible ¼% piggyback on the new sales tax designated for the DECC's UMD arena. Our concerns about negatively affecting the DECC project led us to continue our search.

Our project's spirit endured, and it wasn't long before opportunities began to line up. Alex Giuliani asked Pat Francisco, John Scott, and me to visit the Clyde Iron property he owned in Lincoln Park. After some touring and discussion, we all felt a promising partnership possible.

Meanwhile, ISD 709's high school hockey program needed a more viable home. They'd relied on the DECC to provide practice and game times. But as the DECC pursued more convention and entertainment events, this arrangement grew more difficult each year. Our project piqued the School District's interest. These two opportunities prompted us to rethink the project's scope, consider the community's long-term needs, and revise our mission and organizational approach.

DECISIONS TAKE SHAPE

Conversations with Alex Giuliani and the School District began to clarify our vision. Alex thought he could either donate or provide at a nominal cost the site we needed — the most exciting development since the journey began.

The Duluth Heritage Sports Center (DHSC) established as a 501c3 nonprofit organization. The DHSC would own, construct, and operate the project through solicited private contributions. The initial board of directors included representation from the city, schools, and DAHA, plus five community members.

We revised our vision:

The Duluth Heritage Sports Center provides our youth with a special place that will, amidst the joy of sport, encourage learning, pursuit of excellence, fair play and respect for all.

View of Seitz and Sill arenas flanking Giuliani Hall after completion.

We expanded our mission:

- Provide learning and growth opportunities for our children;
- Substantially expand the tourism contribution to our economy;
- Provide a home for the men's and women's high school hockey program;
- Strengthen the Duluth economic corridor through Lincoln Park;
- Contribute to the restoration and use of historic buildings;
- Intelligently reuse a dormant brownfield industrial site;
- Stimulate the growth of new economic opportunities in Lincoln Park;
- Unite Duluthians around common vision and benefits.

We redesigned the facility to include a year-round hockey arena and a multi-purpose convertible arena. A refurbished Clyde Iron assembly building housed infrastructure and connected the two arenas.

ON YOUR MARK, GET SET, GO

We announced the revamped DHSC on a cold, drizzly evening at the Clyde Iron building. Not knowing what to expect, we were overwhelmed when more than a thousand Duluthians turned out to hear more and cheer on the effort. We knew we were on the right path.

Many Duluthians pitched in and led efforts to advance the plans:

"My family has been supporting youth sports in Duluth for over 70 years. What we care most about is the development of character in children, now and for generations to come. The Duluth Heritage Sports Center is committed to fulfilling that mission."

—Jerry Fryberger

- Heidi Timm-Bijold managed City of Duluth cooperation as well as applying for State of Minnesota grants to rectify contamination issues on the site.

- Dean Holm, president of DAHA, and Executive Director Clarke Coole, led negotiation toward an operating agreement.

- Tim Meinenger, president of Beacon Bank, embraced the project and provided critical and timely financing and advice.

- Steve Seiler, counsel, advised on all organization formation, tax issues, agreements, third party negotiations, bylaws, articles of incorporation, and initial operating policies.

- Terry Scott, CPA, provided critical operating assumptions, proforma performance parameters, and secure procedures for contributions.

- Keith Dixon, Bill Hanson, and Bill Westholm of ISD 709 provided and promoted ISD agreements and terms of participation.

- Tom Livingston of Pro Video produced a video highlighting the vision and values of the DHSC, which we used extensively in presentations to community groups and potential donors.

During these same months, the Legacy Committee led by Patrick Francisco; Business Committee (Greg Toscano); Corporate Committee (Mark Phillips); and Grass Roots Committee (Steve Lent) dove headlong into the fundraising effort to generate $8 million in private contributions, which would be added to the $5.9 million of public funds dedicated to the project.

The Legacy Committee launched a major public information campaign. We enlisted the support of the *Duluth News Tribune*, Duluth Area Chamber of Commerce, Visitor and Convention Bureau, and WDIO led by George Couture and their parent, Hubbard Communications.

Early on, ten Duluthians pledged $50,000 each as seed money for the effort, and bolstered its credibility, encouraging others to join in contributing. One of our rallying cries – "It's much more than hockey" – emphasized the broader mission and its value to the children, families, and community.

Yet another opportunity emerged as the Boys and Girls Club of the Northland sought a larger facility, and the DHSC had approximately 18,000 square feet in our central building. The Boys and Girls Club of the Northland's CEO, Todd Johnson, and the organization's longtime supporter, Dave Goldberg, agreed on a 20-year lease of our space. Following the lease agreement, Mr. Goldberg made a substantial financial contribution to the Center, marking the project's first large pledge.

The Grass Roots and Business Committees began soliciting the general public, offering personally engraved remembrance bricks for $100, and larger granite plaques for $5,000 and $10,000. These sold very quickly and today fill the lobby of the completed Center. Committee members tabled at events, and dollar by dollar, contributions fueled progress.

One particularly memorable moment happened at the DECC Boat and Sports Show, when an elderly woman approached John Scott, who manned our booth, and gave five dollars, which she said was her lunch money. She grew up near Clyde Iron and supported our efforts.

Duluth Marshall and Duluth East teams lead the National Anthem at the Perkins Frenzy tournament in 2018.

Duluth Heritage Sports Center

AVOIDING POTHOLES AND STAYING ON TRACK

The year 2006 was not all roses and sunshine. A flurry of ideas had expanded our vision and prompted a change in direction. Forces in the youth hockey community grew impatient and felt the Board was overreaching for a project too large.

A City Council-established deadline loomed — with three days left to raise a $1.8 million match to the City's insurance contribution, we came up a million dollars short. I was in Patrick Francisco's office discussing what to do when he received a call from Mitch Sill, who wanted to meet and discuss a possible contribution. We met with Mitch and Elva Sill that afternoon and they offered a $250,000 challenge grant contribution – a generous and unexpected offer.

Having left the meeting early, I was keenly aware of the seemingly impossible task of raising the remaining $750,000 in a single weekend. Later that day, Patrick called to inform me Elva and Mitch had reconsidered and pledged $1 million! Their generous gift changed our course, and we averted the impending failure to meet deadline and subsequent collapse of the project.

David Goldberg, and Mitch and Elva Sill's pledges paved the way for other large donors. By the end of 2006, we had verified $11.3 million in private contributions and grants against a project budget of $15.6 million — an unprecedented achievement for Duluth.

GETTING IT TOGETHER

By the end of 2006, the DHSC had formed a new paradigm around cultivating community values — a paradigm to be tested again.

City Council had set a new deadline requiring construction to begin by July 1. Arranging $15 million in construction and long-term financing in a mere six months seemed like an impossible task. As a retired bank president, I was certain that the DHSC would not qualify for traditional financing. Our nonprofit corporation status was less than a year in existence, we had no financial history, and our funds remained as pledges and grants receivable. Plus, our short timeline required a "design/build" approach, creating the potential for added construction costs.

Enter Pam Kramer and Duluth LISC (Local Initiatives Support Corporation) to the rescue. John Scott, a LISC Board member, urged us to explore an alternative financing mechanism through LISC called tax credit financing. We quickly found the prerequisites of the program fit our project like a glove.

Pam's belief in our vision led to Midwest Minnesota Community Development Corporation (MMCDC) issuing the project $3 million in tax credits. Beacon Bank was favorably inclined to participate, and our largest hurdle to date was resolved.

Meanwhile, as fundraising continued, we had an overwhelming task to reach definitive agreements with several different parties, including:

• Purchase agreement with Clyde Park for the property;

- City of Duluth Development and Operating agreements;

- ISD 709 five-year evergreen agreement;

- DAHA five -ear evergreen agreement;

- Boys and Girls Club 20-year lease agreement;

- Complex lending agreements with MMCDC and Beacon Bank;

- Architectural service agreement with DSGW Architects;

- Construction management services agreement with Kraus Anderson to construct the Center.

PUTTING HERITAGE IN THE HERITAGE CENTER

In early 2007, Anita Stech chaired the Heritage Committee and assembled Laurie Carlson, Rachel Sersha, Rose Hoene, Ted Thompson, Kristen Pless, and Sherri Swenson to build into the Center a lasting presence of Duluth's great hockey and skating heritage.

The committee reached out to the community and was overwhelmed by donated scrapbooks, jerseys, jackets, photos, articles, skates, programs, score sheets, referee gear, etc. They organized, planned, and produced a historical display of Duluth's love of skating and hockey — a herculean task. Thanks to this amazing volunteer effort, visitors to the DHSC are often overwhelmed by the warmth and character of this exhibition.

LET 'ER RIP

By June 2007, we were faced with a decision of "go, or no go." Funds collected, although substantial, still fell short of construction costs. With the city's financial contribution at stake, we issued the go-ahead to Kraus Anderson to begin construction — a risky call, but with full faith of the Board.

Phase I was completed in January 2008, and Phase II commenced. Fundraising could not keep up with construction costs, however, and the project developed a $3 million shortfall. From the heart of the worst recession since the 1930s, the outlook was bleak.

All parties rallied, unwilling to let the project fail. We developed a new plan to pay off the accrued construction cost balance, and completed Phase II on schedule.

Ultimately, the completed center cost approximately $20 million, of which only $3 million was not covered by supporting grants or existing pledges — an incredible result of collective efforts to meet our obligations during a deep national recession.

With the feat of construction done, the center still lacked finishing touches. Harbortown Rotary Club stepped up to sponsor the creation of an entry plaza. Led by DuWayne Holm and Greg Wegler, we were able to raise $175,000 in donated materials and contributions to complete a dramatic and welcoming entrance to the center.

"Our whole interest level is centered on improving the chances for all kids to become good citizens."

—Dave Goldberg

MAKING IT WORK

Jerry DeMeo became president and CEO in 2010 to ensure the DHSC fulfilled its promise to the community. The DHSC Foundation, led by Patrick Francisco, continued to raise contributions used to pay off the remaining $3 million, reduce long-term debt, and provide additional resources to meet center objectives. Over $9 million in private pledges came in – unheard of in Duluth's history.

"I believe that most of the solutions for our country will come from the private sector."

—Herb and Barbara Fritch

In 2016, eight years after opening, the DHSC exited its tax credit financing from MMCDC and successfully refinanced its remaining $2.3 million in debt with then Beacon Bank (now Alerus Bank).

ACHIEVING NEW STATUS

The DHSC received the Minnesota Outstanding Economic Development Award in 2008 as part of Clyde Park's recognition, and received the "Let's Play Hockey" 2014 Award as "Minnesota's Best Example of the Spirit of Hockey."

A new partnership with Essentia Health as a program sponsor has cultivated next-level promotion and the creation of meaningful programs for Lincoln Park, Duluth, and the region. Dr. Dan Nickovich, Dr. David Herman (CEO), Kristi Schmidt and the Essentia Board, found that the center's values and strategic direction aligned with Essentia's focus on promoting wellness and well-being. The center's new name, Essentia Health Duluth Heritage Sports Center (EDHC), represents our commitment to working together in this endeavor.

SECURING THE FUTURE – FULLFILLING THE PROMISE

2017-18 marks the tenth anniversary of the EDHC, an opportunity to expand the delivery of programs that teach and reinforce the fundamental values of citizenship to our youth and Center visitors. We have also initiated a dedicated endowment for fiscal security, buffering operational costs and capital improvements and allowing youth programming expansion and creation.

The creation and development of the EDHC has been an incredible and unique journey.

- The journey began in the ashes of a burned out Peterson arena.

- The EDHC became a $20 million multi-purpose community center for children, families, and community organizations.

- The EDHC is a nonprofit corporation that receives no public operating support, taxes, or levies of any kind, including the hotel/motel/food and beverage tax.

- Over 75% of the construction cost was funded privately – unheard of in Duluth.

- The center never had any paid professional development staff or promotional budget. All efforts to develop the Center were uncompensated volunteers.

- Over 375,000 individuals attend EDHC events and activities each year.

- The EDHC has achieved positive operating results.

- The EDHC is a significant economic driver for Lincoln Park business and the community at large.

- The EDHC creates a place that perpetuates the values of personal responsibility and citizenship, and encourages children to "Shoot for the Moon" in all endeavors and be responsible for their actions. ∎

Richard Loraas is a retired bank president and currently serves as president of the Duluth Heritage Sport Center Foundation. He has served since 2006 as a volunteer executive with the DHSC, including as chairman, CEO, and president.

Essentia Health Duluth Heritage Sports Center
Original Board of Directors and Operating Committees

Board of Directors

Richard Loraas
James Olcott
Wayne Parson
Edward Aamodt

Clarke Coole
Carl Seehus
Mark Emmel
Bill Westholm

Mark Baron
Bryan Flaherty
Mark Krysiak

Marketing

Mike Seyfer
Erica Hanson
Steven Waller
Edd Leist

Controllers

Terry Scott
Kenneth Olson
Cami Hanson

Legacy

Patrick Francisco
Jerry Fryberger
Nick Alworth
Ed Aamodt
Bryan Flaherty
Gordy Seitz

Corporate

Mark Phillips
Jack LaVoy
Jim Roberts
Randy Lasky
Andy McDonough
Alex Giuliani
John Scott

Heritage

Anita Stech
Laurie Carlson
Rachel Sersha
Rose Hoene
Ted Thompson
Kristen Pless
Sherri Swenson

Business

Greg Toscano
Jim Olson
Brian Liberty
Stan Karich
Fritz Wrazidlo
Craig Fellman
David Pollard
Joe Dusek
Jeremy Jeanette
Jason Francisco

Grass Roots

Steve Lent
Jim Johnson
John Moline
Bill Cortes
Nancy Nilsen
Jerry DeMeo
Jim Stebe
Judy & Bob Harvey
Scott Lyons

CHAPTER

17

maurices

BUILDING A BILLION-DOLLAR WOMEN'S FASHION
RETAIL BRAND ROOTED IN HOMETOWN

by George Goldfarb

A small women's fashion store founded in 1931 in downtown Duluth during the Great Depression is now a 1,000-store chain across the United States and Canada, and remains headquartered in Duluth.

As Joel Labovitz, the son of maurices founder E. Maurice Labovitz, shared in the first *The Will and the Way*, maurices' success is based on being "...a great place to work and to shop and is good to and for its communities."

And after more than 85 years, this formula remains. While our ownership has changed, and the retail industry is in the midst of significant change, we have stayed true to putting people first and connecting with and supporting our hometown communities.

I was very fortunate to grow up in Duluth, receive an education at the University of Minnesota – Duluth, and

Kevin White Photography

maurices store landscape has a strong Minnesota and Midwest presence, pictured is the maurices store in Fergus Falls, MN.

find a great job with a great company in the community I love. I started my career at maurices as a tax accounting supervisor in 1985, seven years after the Labovitz family sold maurices to the American Retail Group (ARG), also known to many Duluthians as the Brenninkmeyer family from Holland. At the start of my career at maurices, the company was going through a 100-store acquisition.

Through the years to follow, I assumed many different positions within the company. In 2005 we went through another ownership transition when ARG sold to dressbarn, inc. At the time of the acquisition, maurices could have been sold to a private equity group, which likely would have spun us off or sold us. Another route was to enter a strategic partnership with dressbarn. I advocated strongly for the latter. I was serving as chief financial officer when we joined dressbarn in a strategic partnership. There was ample speculation internally and within the community that the acquisition would prompt maurices headquarters to relocate out of Duluth, but David Jaffe, then-president of dressbarn, inc., was adamant that maurices should remain in Duluth. Much of our success had been based on homegrown talent, and our "home office," as the headquarters is referred to, has rightfully reflected the values of the small to mid-size communities we serve.

I was fortunate to co-lead the company from 2007-09 with Lisa Rhodes, the chief merchandising officer at the time, and I became president of maurices in 2009. Honored to be named president, I made a commitment to sustain the "people first" culture. I believed doing the right thing would always create the best results.

In 2011, the parent company, dressbarn, inc., changed its name to ascena retail group, inc. to better represent the various women's brands in its portfolio: maurices, dressbarn, and Justice. The name change also positioned the company for future acquisitions: Lane Bryant and Catherines in 2012; and Ann Taylor, Loft, and Lou & Grey in 2015. The financial strength and resources of ascena, coupled with a strong growth strategy, doubled maurices' sales between 2006 and 2015 ($424 million to over $1 billion) and more than doubled its store count (546 to 951). The beauty was we were able to operate as an independent brand and leverage the strength of a larger company to invest in the infrastructure for future growth.

In 2012, shortly after maurices expanded into Canada, we realized we were quickly outgrowing our current home office in downtown

> I'm proud of our steadfast and longstanding commitment to Duluth and our communities, and ensuring maurices continues to be the best place to work.

maurices new headquarters in downtown Duluth reflects the values of the women and communities it serves and its "people first" culture. Top photo: The "Front Porch" located on each floor of the building is a great example of the inspirational and collaborative spaces available to its associates.

Duluth. Operating out of four separate buildings wasn't efficient and didn't meet our current (and growing) business needs. We explored options to renovate or relocate within Duluth or within our ascena portfolio and landed on a space in downtown Duluth just a few blocks from where we were founded. The former KDAL building on West Superior Street presented an opportunity for redevelopment. A new maurices headquarters would revitalize the western downtown and solidify maurices' commitment to Duluth — a win-win for the company and the community.

Three years in the making, the new maurices headquarters at 425 West Superior Street houses our 400 home office associates and is the largest commercial development in downtown Duluth. The $80-million project was funded with approximately $60 million from maurices and $10 million from the City of Duluth. The Minnesota Department of Employment and Economic Development (DEED) matched the City's $10 million with a grant in support of a much needed public parking ramp and skywalk infrastructure. This was a great example of how a strong, collaborative private-public partnership can benefit the community.

The building spans an entire city block, sits 11 stories tall and is nearly 200,000 square feet. With spectacular views of our city and Lake Superior throughout the building, it's an inspiring place to work.

We also designed the building to promote wellbeing, collaboration, and flexibility in how we work. The building was designed to fit in with the architecture of other downtown buildings, but also serve as a beacon for investment and belief in Duluth.

The home office includes a fitness center; on-site café; outdoor terrace to enjoy fresh air; a large family room for dining, working, or socializing; front porch gathering spaces; and lots of windows to enjoy natural daylight and breathtaking views. With a mindset of openness and transparency, there are no "corner offices." Instead, all associates have window views and natural daylight. To honor our company's hometown heritage, each conference room bears the name of a community where we have a maurices store. Our building is LEED Silver certified, our project was named in the Top 100

Projects of 2016 by *Finance & Commerce*, and it was featured on the cover of *Architecture Minnesota*.

While we've expanded over the years, I'm proud of our steadfast and longstanding commitment to Duluth and our communities, and ensuring maurices continues to be the best place to work. Providing a great work environment also transcends our employees, to our customers, and makes us one of the best places to shop. I'm also proud of our commitment to giving back. Every year we hold our "Best Day Ever," in which we close the office and dedicate half a day to volunteering in the community. Additionally, we dedicate resources toward empowering the lives of women and children. As an example, the maurices "Community Clinic" at the College of St. Scholastica provides training for students and free services to the community. We support children and women at risk through education, and health and wellbeing projects. Our associates uphold our company values, and in turn, our success.

Retail is changing rapidly — as online shopping grows, mall traffic declines — and retailers are transforming their business models. Despite these challenges, the talented people at maurices and ascena continue to innovate and thrive in this most challenging retail environment. Today, maurices has 1,000 stores and 9,000 associates across the U.S. and Canada. We are able to leverage ascena retail group's (a $7-billion powerhouse) infrastructure and systems to support our growth and keep our business healthy. And it all began with a small family-owned store on the northeast corner of 3rd Avenue West and Superior Street (where Wells Fargo bank is today) — this is a great Duluth hometown story. ∎

George Goldfarb is president & CEO of maurices, a women's specialty retailer headquartered in Duluth, MN. Having held various leadership positions with maurices over the past 30 years, George has helped grow maurices into a North American success story with a niche in small town America. A Duluth native, he also is deeply committed to his community, serving on several nonprofit and for-profit boards of directors and has been recognized by many organizations for his leadership.

CHAPTER

18

Pier B Resort Hotel

TURNING CEMENT DUST INTO COMMUNITY GOLD

by Sanford "Sandy" Hoff and Alessandro "Alex" Giuliani

On an overcast Duluth day, Sanford Hoff and Alessandro Giuliani – two Duluth developers who had been friends since their days in the UMD business school – climbed 100' up the stairs to the top of the silos at Pier B and threw open the windows. An extraordinary view of the Duluth cityscape and its harbor greeted them.

It was 2009, and Lafarge Cement Company, who owned half of the industrial waterfront property, was looking to sell. The other half of the property was owned by the Duluth Economic Development Authority (DEDA). The complete site was 7.4 acres, 2,100 feet of shoreline, with Slip 2 to the East and Slip 3 to the west.

The four joined silos had stood sentinel since 1920, when they were built by the Huron Portland Cement Company to store powdered cement, which they sucked from the ships and stored until it was shipped elsewhere to use for

(Above) Site prior to Pier B development.

(Right) The beginning of demolition, removing the "bag house" where powdered cement, stored in the silos, was once bagged for transport.

The silos still stand, a steady emblem of the Duluth waterfront's history and evolution and a nostalgic, prominent fixture in the pier's new image.

making concrete.

Hoff and Giuliani saw the potential of this diamond in the rough – a vision for what it could be, what it could offer the Duluth community and its visitors.

But bringing the possibility of Pier B into reality was an accomplishment that could only come about through an incredible partnering of public and private enterprises. During an economic recession, Hoff and Giuliani assembled a private team of local investors to fund a hospitality project. The pair forged relationships and united a long roster of public agencies, including the U.S. Army Corp of Engineers, Fish and Wildlife, Minnesota Pollution Control Agency (MPCA), the United States Environmental Protection Agency (EPA), State Historical Preservation Office, Duluth City Council, Duluth Economic Development Authority (DEDA), Minnesota Department of Employment and Economic Development (DEED), the Department of Natural Resources, the U.S. Coast Guard, Customs and Border Patrol, and more.

In one of the most complicated private redevelopment projects Duluth has ever seen, multiple visions for this waterfront property – considering all the agencies and the greater Duluth community – merged to become Pier B Resort, Duluth's first upscale waterfront resort with year-round water access and activities.

One of the first tasks Hoff and Giuliani faced was to approach the Duluth Economic Development Authority, who owned the east part of the property, and garner their support and partnership. Mayor Don Ness and his team enthusiastically committed to the opportunity.

Work began to explore the possibilities and challenges of the property. Eric Dott, senior hydrogeologist at Barr Engineering, advised on the development of the waterfront location. The comprehensive land use plan – the overriding land development instrument used by the City of Duluth – zoned the property for waterfront industrial use. To develop the property, the City would have to change the comprehensive land use plan and the underlying zoning. A small area study plan was required, initiated by the Duluth Planning Department, to explore if the land could be shifted to a mixed-use property. This process took many months and much public

Waterfront Redevelopment

RESTORING AN UNSOUND, CONTAMINATED
WATERFRONT FOR NEW USE

by Heidi Timm-Bijold

The configuration of Duluth's waterfront is vastly different today than its pre-industrial origin. Beginning in the late 1800s and continuing into the early 1900s, Duluth's waterfront — largely shallow marshland at that time — was systematically "filled in" to create more land for commercial activity and to facilitate rail and shipping transportation of goods. The fill material included soils of unknown origin, wood and concrete debris — just about anything that provided bulk to build surface. Thriving industry dictated this approach to land expansion. Pile on unregulated industrial practices of the time, and we are left with legacy issues we must address in all of today's waterfront redevelopment.

Courtesy of City of Duluth

View of the industrial waterfront property that is now home to properties including Pier B Resort, as seen from atop The Seventh Avenue West Incline Railway that operated between 1890 and 1939. The water on the left side is the slip between today's Pier B and Bayfront.

input. Hoff and Giuliani also held area planning meetings, reaching out to various community organizations to share their vision for the property and hear community reactions. The community responded with a wide range of ideas for Pier B – everything from rain gardens to go-kart tracks to mini putt-putt golf courses.

A vision for the property emerged. Hoff and Giuliani saw a gap in Duluth's hospitality market; while Canal Park had developed into a tremendously successful hospitality corridor, Duluth was missing a resort with waterfront access.

John Cook, an imaginer with Disney who worked on the Epcot Center development in Florida, was hired to help with initial site planning and concept design. An early idea was to make the iconic silos into the hotel. The silos are structurally sound, but contractors and experts cited uncertainty about cost and functionality, and recommended keeping the silos for their historic value and building a separate hotel.

Another challenge was the environmental issues associated with the property. This brownfield redevelopment project was one of the first public/private partnerships for an environmental remediation project to include land and underwater work, requiring some creative, cost-effective solutions to clean contaminated slips.

Slips in the estuary are contaminated and mandated to be cleaned by the Minnesota Pollution Control Agency. Because the

WATERFRONT REDEVELOPMENT

Those legacy issues range from environmental contamination on land and in adjacent water bodies; to unstable soils; to long-neglected seawalls and pier facings that may be allowing contaminated soil to erode into the harbor; to construction challenges often unanticipated until a project is underway.

In this chapter about the Pier B project, we read about using clean harbor dredge material to cap the contaminated material at the bottom of Slip 2. But did you know that, due to the shallow water table of the site, utilities were installed by divers?

Another waterfront redevelopment project of recent years, the Canal Park Brewing Company, faced brownfield challenges not due to the former operation at that site, but rather, the fill material brought in by the City in the early 1900s to expand the land base. One hundred plus years later, we learned the fill was contaminated. Upon that

Continued on page 153

(Top) Silos Restaurant and Pier B Resort Hotel viewed from the city side.

(Bottom) Today's Pier B viewed from the harbor side. Resort and restaurant guests have easy access to a boat launch and boat slip rentals.

cleanup of Slip 2 could not be completed in time for Pier B's opening, the property development team took it upon themselves to finance and arrange for its remediation using sand from the harbor dredged by the U.S. Army Corp of Engineers to cap the contaminated soils. Originally, the slip was 18-25 feet deep; after capping with sand, it stands at 10-12 feet deep. Pier B now has a clean bill of health upland and in the slip. Getting the dredged material saved the project $750,000, and saved the contractors from having to pay to haul the material out of the area. Additionally, since the Minnesota Pollution Control Agency was charged with cleaning the slip at a cost of $3 million, plus 3-4 years of work, the public/private partnership saved the State of Minnesota millions of dollars and years of work.

Heidi Timm- Bijold of the City of Duluth/DEDA, who assists developers in remediating brownfield (contaminated) sites, was instrumental in obtaining two DEED grants worth almost $2 million dollars, crucial in helping this project succeed.

Pier B resort officially opened on Friday, June 18, 2016 – Grandma's Marathon weekend.

The resort offers an exceptional vantage point; it overlooks the working harbor, the hillside cityscape, the Lift Bridge and the Big Lake beyond. The lakeside patio fire pit gathers guests outdoors, and the event center, boardroom, and private rooftop deck overlooking the harbor host many weddings and events.

WATERFRONT REDEVELOPMENT
Continued from page 151

discovery, it was excavated and replaced with clean fill. Then when the brewery opened in late 2012, one of its inaugural beers was an IPA called "Clean Dirt," paying homage to the remediation efforts it took to clean up and redevelop the site.

We see redevelopment projects come to life along our waterfront, but what most of us *don't* see are the extraordinary expectations those projects must meet to make it. Resolving legacy issues often proves expensive and challenging, and requires creativity and public financing partnerships to get it done. Regulatory entities fulfill their individual missions to ensure projects adhere to important standards, but the missions don't necessarily align. Historic Preservation, for instance, may require a solid, linear seawall rebuilt to match its original 1910 structure; at the same time, Habitat Restoration may require a softened

Continued next page

CLEAN LEGACY
Continued from previous page

seawall to encourage fish spawning. The expectation of each regulatory entity, considered on its own merit and mission, is understandable. Responding to the constellation of expectations, however, is undoubtedly daunting.

We are diligent in our efforts to remedy the legacy issues from our past, and we hold high standards for the legacy we leave for the future. We are living a critical chapter in Duluth's story, a chapter of reconciling past and future — it's complicated, it's important, and we are getting it done. ∎

The private harbor offers more than 20 boat slips and a boat launch for use by resort and restaurant guests. Guests also put in kayaks, canoes, and paddleboards. Boaters can tie up and dine at the Silos restaurant. The indoor pool overlooks the harbor, and the outdoor hot tub is open year-round for a truly unique experience.

Pedestrians walking the city Bayfront path can cross a bridge and continue around Slip 2. Slip 2 presents a year-round outdoor experience for its guests, with a small skating rink and ice golf course in the winter, and a yurt with a fireplace just beyond that.

And the iconic silos? They were kept as-is, holding many possibilities for the future – from condominiums to retail to an ice climbing wall. The private and public partnerships behind Pier B's success have proven the property's creative potential and ability to surprise. ∎

Heidi Timm-Bijold is the manager of the city's Business Development Department. She serves as a project manager for both the city and DEDA in projects that often involve varying aspects of contamination cleanup, redevelopment and infrastructure challenges. She also serves on the board of Minnesota Brownfields. Heidi adopted the community of Duluth in 1983 and will be forever grateful for the path that brought her here.

Sandy Hoff is a native Duluthian and the co-developer of Pier B Resort Hotel. He is president of F.I. Salter Co. Inc. and co-owner of a variety of small regional businesses.

Alessandro Giuliani was raised and lives in Duluth and was a co-developer of Pier B Resort Hotel. He has also developed other local properties in the community, including Clyde Park. He owns and operates Clyde Iron Works Restaurant and Event Center.

CHAPTER

19

Atlas Industrial Park

INVESTING IN BROWNFIELD'S NEXT LIFE
WITH GRIT AND DETERMINATION

by Heidi Timm-Bijold

The story of Duluth's renaissance strings together its booming industrial past, decline in light of a dying industrial era, reconciliation of legacy problems, and a bright, budding modern industrial future. The work to bridge two industrial eras is arduous, rewarding, and vital to Duluth's ongoing prosperity. And the work to forge a cleaner legacy is likewise, arduous, rewarding, and vital.

ONE HUNDRED YEARS AGO, in 1918, the Atlas Cement Plant was in full operation. Built by U.S. Steel to take the slag by-product of iron-making to produce cement for its use in concrete, the cement plant first went into production in 1916.

NINETY YEARS AGO, in 1928 and leading up to the 1929 recession, operations at the steel mill and cement plant reached capacity, with 400 workers employed at the cement plant. Operations peaked once again in the 1940s, both during and immediately after World War II.

The Atlas Universal Cement Plant in the '50s or '60s, likely photographed from Bardon's Peak looking eastward. U.S. Steel Duluth Works steel mill and Spirit Lake on the lower St. Louis River appear in the background.

FORTY YEARS AGO, in 1978, the "Gary-New Duluth Neighborhood Plan" was published. The cement plant was now closed and steel plant operations were phasing out. Residents of Gary-New Duluth were heartened by the investment of new housing in their neighborhoods as well as a community-wide interest in expanding recreational opportunities within the St. Louis River. Should heavy industry once again be encouraged to concentrate here? This transition warranted a plan.

FIFTEEN YEARS AGO, in 2003, the Duluth Economic Development Authority purchased the 62-acre cement plant site for $232,000 with the goal of cleaning up the contaminated site and establishing an industrial park.

TEN YEARS AGO, in 2008, the IKONICS Corporation completed their expansion at the Atlas Industrial Park.

TODAY, in 2018, ten years after the IKONICS expansion to the Atlas Industrial Park, they remain the only occupant. What has transpired in these last ten years? To understand that answer, I need to return to the beginning — to the late 1800s.

Northeast Minnesota Historical Center (Robert Young, Duluth 1951)

U.S. Steel Duluth Works site, Morgan Park 1951.

In 1891 Gary was incorporated as a City, and the Village of New Duluth was formed. The 1890s was a decade of anticipation with increased rail service introduced along these river-bound neighborhoods that were already the epicenter of Duluth's heavy industry. In 1907 U.S. Steel announced their intention to build a steel plant in Duluth and formed a subsidiary, the Minnesota Steel Company. Morgan Park was built as a company town for those who worked at the steel plant. A global industry leader, U.S. Steel subsidiaries included over half of the state's mines on the Iron Range and a fleet of Great Lakes ore boats. Ore docks and iron-ore distribution rail yards were owned by the Duluth, Missabe and Northern (DM&N) and Duluth and Iron Range (D&IR) railways, both of which were headquartered in Duluth and were U. S. Steel subsidiaries. Minnesota Steel (the steel mill) opened in 1915 and the Universal Portland Cement plant opened the following year, both serviced by company rail at Steelton. Note: Universal Portland Cement merged with Universal Atlas Cement in 1930 — hence the name "Atlas" in moving forward.

The common ownership by U.S. Steel of the steel plant, cement plant and railroad over 100 years ago contributes to the complexity of redeveloping those sites today.

At one time in history these combined U.S. Steel operations employed an estimated 1 of every 13 employed in Duluth — Minnesota Steel alone reached 3,600 employees. Peak employment at Atlas reached 400 men who could produce 4,000 barrels of cement daily. Portland cement, lime and plaster production occurred on the 62-acre site filled with approximately 20 structures. One of those structures contained 67 silos for storing cement. Lime rock milling, gypsum and slag blending, and cement-making kiln processes were all located on the northern half of the property. Bulk material delivery and storage areas with a network of on-site rail lines were primarily located on the southern half of the property. The plant used state-of-the-art technology intended to reduce the dust generated by the cement production process.

Within ten years of operating (yes, as early as 1930!) the *Duluth News Tribune* reported on the environmental decline of the St. Louis River attributed to the Minnesota Steel operation. A far different form of contamination — that of air quality — was caused by dust from the cement plant. As an excerpt from the 1978 "Gary-New Duluth Neighborhood Plan" explains:

> *After its (cement plant) closure, the air quality improved in the Gary-Morgan Park area due primarily to the absence of dust which no longer was emitted from the stacks. The (Minnesota) Pollution Control Agency has estimated.... approximately 90 pounds of dust per hour....All of this contributed to a gray powder covering everything in the area.*

And so, when the City of Duluth's Planning Department, with a steering committee comprised of community and industry members, commenced with the plan that was published in September 1978, Gary-New Duluth was taking on a discussion echoed elsewhere in Rust Belt communities around the Great Lakes during the chapter in national history remembered as deindustrialization. And it is that chapter that continues to be rewritten at the Atlas Industrial Park.

I want to stop this narrative for a moment to acknowledge the scores upon scores of families in Duluth whose family members once worked for one of these U.S. Steel companies. I know the immense pride I have as a woman who grew up on a southeastern Minnesota dairy farm of fourth-generation ancestry. I have witnessed the pride of those whose relatives once worked at Clyde Iron Works who now walk into the restaurant at Clyde Park and see images of ancestors. Those who once worked at Minnesota Steel or Atlas did not make the decisions that led to sites compromised by contamination and other impediments. It is our opportunity, in the current chapter, to restore pride to those family members.

Structures and infrastructure at Atlas were decommissioned and abandoned and eventually bulldozed to the ground. Former underground utility lines were kept in place; fill consisting of slag, rock, bricks, wood, concrete debris and asphalt was placed at the site when the site was re-graded. We came to learn, years later, that the filling and re-grading moved contaminated material to unsuspected locations on the site and also destroyed any semblance of storm water drainage systems that had once been in place. That site work was done when U.S. Steel still owned Atlas, the steel plant, and the DM&IR property sandwiched between them.

The work to bridge two industrial eras is arduous, rewarding, and vital to Duluth's ongoing prosperity.

IKONICS

VENERABLE DULUTH SPECIALIST EXPANDS

by Michael Sullivan

It was a bitter-cold and windy Duluth day on May 1, 2008 when IKONICS Corporation broke ground at Atlas Industrial Park (Atlas), the former Atlas Cement Plant, thereby marking both a new chapter for IKONICS and a stride toward the burgeoning modern industrial vision for western Duluth. The expansion fortified the company's Duluth roots and built on a partnership to remediate and revive the erstwhile industrial site.

(top left) Bill Ulland and Don Ness

(top right) Jim Stauber and Dan McElroy join Ulland and Ness, breaking ground at Atlas Industrial Park. (2008)

(bottom) IKONICS manufacturing center can be seen from Commonwealth Avenue.

Actions taken at one of the company-owned properties was not objectionable to another company property, even with unintended consequences.

Property ownership has in fact changed, and that has provided significant challenges in the revitalization of the Atlas property. The DM&IR property is now owned by the Canadian National (CN) Railway. Atlas is now owned by the Duluth Economic Development Authority (DEDA). The Minnesota Steel site remains under the ownership of U.S. Steel; they are actively engaged with several public partners in the remediation of the steel mill site, and more imminent, the cleanup of contaminated sediments in the St. Louis River at Spirit Lake.

I believe it is true to say that the DEDA Commissioners who approved the purchase of the former cement plant site in late 2003 could not have fully understood or appreciated the journey ahead to bring the site back to productive use. I also believe it is true that, had DEDA not purchased the site and embarked upon a methodical journey towards site remediation and revitalization, it would still be a blighted 62-acre site behind a chain link/barbed wire fence. DEDA's undertaking of the Atlas site is an example of the unique role we, versus the private sector, can assume.

DEDA owned the Atlas site for several years before discussions began in earnest with Bill Ulland and Claude Piguet of the Duluth-based company IKONICS about

IKONICS

The story of IKONICS' expansion to Atlas began in the early 2000s when IKONICS CEO Bill Ulland declared the company had outgrown its Grand Avenue location. Ulland's new business initiatives required a new location, and his long-term goal was to move all IKONICS operations to a single campus. Thus, the search for additional land began.

Meanwhile, the Duluth Economic Development Authority (DEDA) had purchased the former Atlas Cement Plant site in the Morgan Park neighborhood of Duluth in hopes of one day reversing the site's demise and putting it back to good and productive use.

A few years passed, and then an opportune partnership began to take shape.

In the fall of 2007, IKONICS announced that DEDA had approved an agreement giving the company the option to purchase approximately 15 acres at the Atlas site. With new business

Continued on page 163

Aerial view of the abandoned Atlas site, pre-cleanup.

their need to expand beyond their primary facility. They identified eleven acres understood to have the least amount of contamination. With environmental technical assistance from two firms, Environmental Troubleshooters and Barr Engineering, and with financial assistance from the Minnesota Department of Employment and Economic Development (DEED)'s competitive cleanup grant program as well as from DEDA, the site was remediated (under budget), and IKONICS began operations at Atlas.

During that period of time City staff was increasingly engaged in discussions with staff from the Environmental Protection Agency (EPA)'s Region 5 office in Chicago. When they became more aware of Duluth's brownfields challenges to include the Atlas site, a remarkable City/EPA partnership began to take shape that continues

Courtesy of City of Duluth

to this day. In the case of Atlas, EPA sent a consultant team in 2009 to further assess the remaining 51 acres, and based on those findings, DEDA applied for and was awarded an EPA cleanup grant in 2011. In 2011-12, DEDA was successful in securing DEED infrastructure grant funding to extend utilities throughout the site and to expand the roadways. A concurrent DEED cleanup grant funded cleanup needed during construction of the infrastructure. In 2014, EPA provided a Green Infrastructure grant to the City — a portion of which was used

IKONICS
Continued from page 161

initiatives on the horizon, the proposed site was the only available location in Duluth that would support both of Ulland's main goals — to eventually house all operations on one campus and to remain in Duluth.

By the time of the groundbreaking ceremony in 2008, IKONICS and DEDA had sealed the deal for the company's expansion at Atlas, ushering in a public/ private partnership to embark on site remediation, readying the land for redevelopment. The move had melded Ulland's goals for IKONICS with a broader vision, which was gaining momentum, to revitalize the western half of Duluth, comprised of neighborhoods long fatigued by the remnants of a waned industrial era. Modern industry could help restore prosperity to these neighborhoods.

Local leaders celebrated with IKONICS — DEDA's executive director, Tom Cotruvo, and its

Continued on page 165

Excavating for installation of utilities at Atlas.

Appearing rather inconspicuous, this pond was created as a pilot (successful) stormwater management tool at Atlas.

at Atlas to construct proper storm water drainage. The EPA, in 2016, once again offered up a consultant team to study and identify potential solutions to the concerns that result when storm water interacts with the residual cement kiln dust remaining in the foundations of the former 67 silos that had been razed. To be clear: this has been a methodical journey made possible by DEDA's tenacity, EPA's commitment to full site revitalization, and DEED's critical grant funding programs.

We have also benefited from rich, local partnerships.

DEDA was approached by staff from the University's Natural Resources Research Institute (NRRI) in 2011 about a research project they were undertaking in partnership with the U.S. Army Corps of Engineers to study potential beneficial applications of dredged material taken from our harbor. The concept was to use this material to construct a pilot stormwater pond with the goal of neutralizing the high pH present in surface water at the site. If successful, DEDA recognized this as a long-term solution to managing the volume of stormwater that cascades down the steep hillside onto Atlas before leaving the site; remember, no longer can that water continue to flow onto the once U.S. Steel-owned railway and steel plant properties. The pilot pond performed splendidly and in years subsequent, DEDA has partnered with the Duluth Seaway Port Authority and local contractors to have dredge material and excess construction

IKONICS
Continued from page 163

board president, Duluth City Councilor Jim Stauber, enthusiastically supported the company's expansion, and then-Mayor Don Ness praised DEDA and IKONICS for the work invested in finalizing the purchase and planning for future development. "This is a good story for Duluth, all the way around," Ness said.

IKONICS benefited from the state's Job Opportunity Building Zone (JOBZ) initiative, a Minnesota Department of Employment and Economic Development (DEED) program designed to offer tax incentives to companies whose expansions result in job creation in Greater Minnesota. Minnesota DEED commissioner at the time, Dan McElroy, said at the groundbreaking, "This is the sort of initiative the JOBZ program was engineered to support...IKONICS is a long-standing, well-respected corporate citizen and employer in Duluth

Continued on page 167

Atlas Industrial Park viewed from Bardon's Peak overlook in late spring of 2018.
Commonwealth Avenue runs through the foreground; and Spirit Lake, in the background.

project soils transported to our site for its reclamation. Cavernous, open foundations have been filled, storm water drainage has been designed and constructed, things have greened up and the site no longer looks forlorn.

We even had, on two occasions, offers from the U.S. Army Reserve and the National Guard to provide heavy equipment assistance on the site as professional training for their soldiers. Neither came to be, but I think it's testimony to the possibilities that difficult journeys bring about.

In thinking about the last several years, I see an alignment of efforts by other agencies that contributes also to a positive future for the Atlas Industrial Park: City business development staff secured supplemental funds to the Minnesota Department of Transportation's

Jason Hale, City of Duluth

IKONICS
Continued from page 165

and it is gratifying to see it expanding its business and supporting new jobs for the local economy."

The first phase of IKONICS' expansion at Atlas included a 35,000-square-foot manufacturing center and warehouse. IKONICS West, as its known internally, became operational in 2009 and houses IKONICS Advanced Material Solutions, serving the aerospace and electronics industries with non-traditional precision abrasive machining, a combination of IKONICS' core technologies used to perorate composites and other brittle materials; and IKONICS Industrial Inkjet Solutions, performing next-generation digital texturing, a revolutionary process of placing texture foils into molds, producing greater resolution and improved image stability and speed at a lower cost than traditional texture-making methods.

In 2016 IKONICS

Continued on next page

(MnDOT) 2015-16 rehabilitation of Highway 23/Commonwealth Avenue for enhancements, such as sidewalks that now extend along the Atlas site. The CN Railway invested over $30 million in the construction of double trackage that run along the southern boundary of Atlas; that project included rebuilding the rail bridge across Commonwealth to a height that now accommodates truck traffic from Commonwealth to Becks Road and then to I-35. These efforts collaterally improve connectivity to the Atlas site.

IKONICS

Continued from previous page

announced its second phase of expansion to include a production facility. Duluth Mayor Emily Larson joined several City of Duluth and DEDA officials at the ribbon cutting. Johnson Wilson Constructors, general contractor for the project, along with LHB Engineers and other subcontractors were also on hand.

IKONICS had grown and returned a new form of industry to western Duluth, paying homage to a once booming era of American labor. ∎

Michael Sullivan is the marketing manager for IKONICS Corporation. After graduating from UMD with a degree in business management and political science, Michael joined the imaging industry in 1996. He currently manages the Marketing Department for IKONICS Corporation divisions, including IKONICS Imaging, Chromaline Screen Print Products, IKONICS Advanced Materials Solutions and IKONICS Industrial Inkjet Solutions.

It is now 2018. DEDA staff are actively marketing the seven parcels available at a time when western Duluth is experiencing tremendous investment in river cleanup, trail expansions and other recreational amenities. Housing projects driven by the private sector are taking shape. Economic development does not occur in a vacuum; it requires the right mix of amenities, housing, logistics. Companies invest in communities that invest in themselves. DEDA and its multiple partners have invested in Atlas for what I believe is an important next chapter in our community's unfolding legacy. ∎

Heidi Timm-Bijold is the manager of the City's Business Development Department. She serves as a project manager for both the city and DEDA in projects that often involve varying aspects of contamination cleanup, redevelopment and infrastructure challenges. She also serves on the board of Minnesota Brownfields. Heidi adopted the community of Duluth in 1983 and will be forever grateful for the path that brought her here.

AUTHOR ACKNOWLEDGMENTS

Alanen, Arnold R. *Morgan Park: Duluth, U.S. Steel, and the Forging of a Company Town.* University of Minnesota Press, 2007.

Dierckins, Tony and Norton, Maryanne C. *Lost Duluth.* Zenith City Press, 2012.

Gary-New Duluth Neighborhood Plan. City of Duluth with Architectural Resources, Inc., 1978.

NEW LIFE

"There may have been a time
when preservation was about saving an old building here and there,
but those days are gone.
Preservation is in the business of saving communities
and the values they embody."

—Richard Moe,
president of the National Trust for Historic Preservation, 1993-2009;
Duluth native

CHAPTER

20

Clyde Park

NEIGHBORHOOD HEART THROBS AMIDST INDUSTRIAL HERITAGE

by John Erickson and Eric Dott

Synergy: the interaction or cooperation of two or more organizations, substances, or other agents to produce a combined effect greater than the sum of their separate effects. (English by Oxford Dictionaries, 2018.)

To say the Clyde Iron Works site redevelopment is the embodiment of the word "synergy" may be an understatement. Interaction and cooperation, yes, aplenty; but without indescribable community spirit, the outcome would have fallen short of the hub it's become to the neighborhood, and the city.

Alex Giuliani led the extra-synergistic effort that saved Clyde Iron Works from an unceremonious demise. And a group of local youth hockey supporters dared to jump on

West-facing view of the Clyde Iron Works Machine Shop in the early 1920s. Hundreds of windows let in the daylight by which the laborers could easily see to manufacture the state-of-the-art heavy machinery of the day.

board with Alex on a risky, uncertain path toward a vision of a youth sports center at the Clyde site.

To say that Clyde Iron Works history is the embodiment of synergy is possibly an even greater understatement. To appreciate the redevelopment of the site, now anchored by the Clyde Iron Works Restaurant and Event Center and the Essentia Health Duluth Heritage Sports Center, it's important to understand the past.

Established in 1889, the original Clyde Iron Works — Clyde, for short — was a steel foundry and manufacturer of heavy machines, such as the Whirley crane, skidders, yarders, hoists, and derricks used in the booming logging industry. Clyde machinery was once instrumental in completing well-known projects such as the Panama Canal, the Empire State Building, and the Golden Gate Bridge. Throughout World War I and World War II, Clyde was called upon to build equipment necessary for the war effort and employed 500 men at peak wartime.

After WWII, despite a decreased workforce and numerous ownership changes, Clyde remained strong, producing the world's largest portable hoist to pull the lines for New York's 4,200-foot-long Verrazano-Narrows suspension bridge. Orders came in through the 1970s but didn't sustain through the '80s, and the plant closed in 1986 to merge with the marine division of American Hoist & Derrick in St. Paul to become AmClyde. Between 1987 and 2002,

Duluth's transition from old to new industry, and its role in past and future manufacturing, forms an interesting circuitry, as is the case in this story:

IPS Cranes, a Minnesota-based crane manufacturer and refurbisher with a growing presence in West Duluth, purchased the assets of American & Ohio Locomotive Crane Co. in 2017. American & Ohio Locomotive Crane Co. formed when Ohio Locomotive Crane Co. purchased the assets of the locomotive crane division of American Hoist & Derrick, the same company whose marine division merged with Clyde upon Clyde's 1986 closure. By purchasing American & Ohio Locomotive Crane Co., IPS Cranes brought back to Duluth over one million Clyde Iron Works original plans and patterns to be used in continued fabrication at IPS Cranes' Duluth plant.

In other words, Clyde came home. ∎

the 10.5-acre Lincoln Park site was marginally used for various machining and fabricating purposes by multiple owners. The site fell into increasing disrepair and neglect and eventually diminished to tired remains of more than 100 years of Duluth ingenuity, productivity and strength.

In 2003, Alex purchased the then-vacant Clyde Iron Works site. In 2004, the City of Duluth coordinated Phase II environmental site investigation, performed by Barr Engineering Company, to help Alex collect information for potential site redevelopment. The site was deemed a brownfield, which means it had the potential for, or actual, presence of historical soil and/or groundwater contamination, thus making it a brownfield, as opposed to an uncontaminated greenfield. A long history of industrial use had left behind contaminants that would require special mitigation before the property could be used again.

In 2004 Eric Dott, a hydrogeologist with Barr, first met Alex to review the findings of the environmental site assessment work and explain possible grant-funding possibilities. Eric recounts the first and subsequent meetings below.

> *I remember meeting Alex for the first time to discuss the results of an early environmental assessment, I set out to explain the State's brownfields program and various brownfields grant programs. We met in the former nerve center of Clyde Iron Works. The office, filled with historical photos of the plant's machinery and the men who built it, was sparsely furnished with a salvaged old wooden drafting table and blueprint storage cabinet. Across the street, the once-robust manufacturing center stood shuttered.*
>
> *Alex was soft spoken and unassuming. He explained why he bought the site. "I just knew this site would eventually catch the interest of someone," he said, "but if a developer were to buy it, they would likely tear everything down and build a large box store." Alex paused. "I don't think that should happen — just look at these cool old buildings," he said. "A lot of people have worked here, and it holds an important place in this neighborhood's heart. I think it could be turned into something valuable to the community."*

It was easy to see Alex's passion for this place. He explained his vision to create community space — "a place the community will want to come," he described. He asked if I could help him realize this vision.

How could I not be similarly enthused? This site had all the components of an enticing challenge — complex remediation issues, tremendous buildings and rich history, and an owner with a compelling vision and catching community spirit. While Alex didn't yet have a specific end-use nailed down, his gut said to move forward — and he trusted his heart would follow through. I wanted to be part of his team.

We walked the site and peeked into the old buildings that day. Alex told me about his passion for soccer, and that he still played. He hoped to incorporate a place for soccer and other sports, especially during the winter months.

Little did we know, Alex's wish to incorporate sports would usher in an opportune partnership, one that would become the foundation for successful transformation of Clyde Iron Works into today's Clyde Park.

In late 2004, a few blocks away from Clyde, an explosion and fire claimed the city-owned Peterson Arena. Mere days later, the neighborhood and community resolved to fill the void left by the arena's demise. The initial response was to simply replace the destroyed rink, mainly home to neighborhood youth hockey, with a similar structure. But a greater vision emerged. Local businessmen Pat Francisco and John Scott began studying concepts for a new facility — one that would house youth hockey but also provide opportunities beyond hockey. A year passed. A concept had gained traction — a two-sheet ice facility with plentiful seating, locker rooms, concessions, viewing areas, etc. This community-center-like concept garnered support and enthusiasm and outgrew the original Peterson Arena site. The project needed a new home.

A few blocks away sat Clyde, teeming with potential. The ten-acre Clyde site once included as many as 36 buildings, several now gone,

Skilled immigrant and first-generation American laborers were the majority of the workforce at Clyde Iron Works. They brought a variety of smith, carpentry, and construction skills to the plant every day.

and the remainder in disrepair. Buildings of brick and timber, which once housed fabrication and assembly lines, occupied the eastern half of the site. The company's former horse stables — large and wooden and the oldest structure on the site — and some old rail line remnants, occupied the mostly bare western half of the site.

Early conversations about melding the two visions — Clyde and what had become known as the Duluth Heritage Sports Center (DHSC)— prompted a feasibility study. Local firm DSGW Architects had already been hired to complete a sports center design and conducted the feasibility study.

John Scott and John Erickson of DSGW toured the Clyde property with Alex on a cold winter day. The buildings' aged, perforated roofs shed daylight into the pigeon-infested spaces. The challenge would be great, but Alex's vision was clear. He saw beauty in the simplicity of the raw structures — brick, steel, concrete — that spoke of the

A rare 1927 photo of Clyde Iron Works personnel — laborers, foremen, and engineers pictured with gear parts and products made on site.

Industrial Revolution. There was a story to tell. Toes frozen, Alex warmed up to a promising partnership.

Although a two-sheet ice facility with an adjoining indoor soccer pavilion was a good physical fit for the western portion of the Clyde site, further investigation into that piece of the property deemed it unsuitable for a large building project. A storm line ran through that portion of the site, 30 feet underground. Soil borings revealed that wood, industrial slag, scrap materials, and dirt filled what was once a ravine, leveling the site to make room for expanding industrial needs. Save for the completion of an exhaustive, cost-prohibitive land remediation, these factors made clear that a new site option was needed.

2005 came to a close. An alternative placement of the sports center emerged. The relatively clean and nearly redevelopment-ready southeastern edge of the property included a large fabrication building and an adjacent row of buildings associated with Duluth Brewing

Three Irish Sisters

Wedding ceremony and reception of Antonia Giuliani and Beau Hughes, held at the historical Clyde Iron Works Event Center on December 31, 2016.

& Malting. Although the space could accommodate the proposed sports center, it would require a move that Alex was leery to make: demolition of a building that possessed redevelopment potential.

This revelation placed the entire development on a fulcrum. Was this the right partnership and vision for the property? Alex revisited his original goal: creating a place where the community would want to come. This partnership felt right; this vision felt right, both for Clyde and the community.

The beginning of 2006 brought refreshed vision and renewed momentum. Synergy between multiple entities awakened to support the trajectory of the project. Two ice sheets would flank a historic centerpiece Clyde Iron Works building. The dynamic redevelopment would weave the story of Clyde's heritage with the story of Duluth's hockey heritage. Working with the City of Duluth's business resource manager, Heidi Timm-Bijold, four brownfield grants totaling more than $2.2 million were secured, including grants from the U.S. Environmental Protection Agency and the Minnesota

State Department of Employment and Economic Development for environmental cleanup work.

Alex agreed to donate to the DHSC, which by this time had taken up as a nonprofit organization, the land for the arena and pavilion and the land for parking. He also donated the centerpiece building, now aptly named Giuliani Hall, which connects the two arenas. Alex's donation of the land and building provided a significant financial boost to the DHSC project and cemented a path forward.

The Duluth School District, the Duluth Amateur Hockey Association, and the Boys and Girls Club of the Northland all became key supporting entities, and the Duluth Heritage Sports Center came to fruition at Clyde Park. The Duluth Children's Museum later moved onto the site, rounding out the space as a true community center.

Alex renovated the cornerstone Clyde building at the corner of 29th Avenue West and Michigan Street and opened Clyde Iron Works Restaurant and Event Center there in the spring of 2010. The renovation keeps Clyde's heritage intact. A giant bridge crane hovers over the new brick, wood-fired ovens in a commercial kitchen designed to serve the restaurant and its sizable catering business. A huge photomural of Clyde foundry workers faces a now-popular neighborhood watering hole on the restaurant's upper mezzanine. Clyde Park's event center is the most heavily used community space in town. In keeping with his vision of "a place the community will

> This revelation placed the entire development on a fulcrum. Was this the right partnership and vision for the property? Alex revisited his original goal: creating a place where the community would want to come.

want to come," Alex is generous in providing the space for events benefiting the community. The silence of once humming machinery has been replaced with sounds of weddings, music shows, and friends gathering together to rediscover Clyde and its place in our city. ∎

John Erickson is a principal at DSGW Architects in Duluth. He has three decades of architectural experience, working on a wide variety of education, commercial and nonprofit projects in Duluth and the surrounding region. After the destruction of the Peterson Arena to a fire, John took on the role of lead architect to assist Alex Giuliani in developing the Clyde site. He worked closely with the Duluth community to plan and develop the Duluth Heritage Sports Center.

Eric Dott is a vice president at Barr Engineering Company. He has nearly three decades of experience as a hydrogeologist and environmental consultant. He became involved in the Clyde redevelopment project by helping Alex Giuliani with environmental assessment, remediation, and development planning, and his role quickly expanded to joining the development team in seeking and securing brownfield grant funding for the project. Eric's clients have included industrial, developer, property management, legal, county, municipal, and nonprofit clients. He lives in Duluth with his wife and two children.

AUTHOR ACKNOWLEDGMENTS

Project Partners:

Alessandro Giuliani, Clyde Park, Inc.

Barr Engineering

Boys and Girls Club

City of Duluth

Donors of all stations, of all amounts

DSGW Architects

Duluth Amateur Hockey Association

Duluth Heritage Sports Center

Independent School District 709

Kraus-Anderson Construction Company

Kraus-Anderson Mortgage Company

Local Banks

Local Initiatives Support Corporation (LISC)

Minnesota Community Capital Fund

Minnesota Department of Employment and Economic Development (DEED)

Minnesota Pollution Control Agency (MPCA)

National Trust for Historic Preservation

Northspan

The Volunteers, The "Soul Warriors"

U.S. Environmental Pollution Agency

Zeppa Foundation

CHAPTER

21

Great Lakes Aquarium Catches Its Wave!

by Jack LaVoy

Great Lakes Aquarium represents a turnaround story of a facility that went from being a community concern, to emerge in the unchallenged position as Duluth's number-one, paid premier attraction. The aquarium's success illustrates what can be accomplished through leadership, creativity and a collaborative, community team effort.

Great Lakes Aquarium at Lake Superior Center first opened to the public on July 29, 2000, to great fanfare and with huge expectations — expectations driven, in part, by unrealistic attendance and revenue projections developed by project consultants. By the second half of 2002, it became clear that the anticipated attendance levels could not be sustained and that more cash was needed for operations than was being generated by its income.

This set of circumstances created a series of political crises that ultimately led to contracting out the aquarium's operations to Ripley's Leisure Entertainment in 2003, an arrangement into which both parties entered with completely different sets of expectations. The City of Duluth was desirous to simply turn the facility over to Ripley's and end the city's financial involvement, and Ripley's saw it as an opportunity to develop a template for acquiring marginally performing, publicly owned operations and securing public financial assistance to turn them around and grow the business.

Ultimately, those contrary sets of expectations led to ongoing levels of friction and frustration between the two partners, until in late summer 2007, Ripley's terminated the relationship. At that point, the decision was made to return operations to local control, and I was recruited to serve as the aquarium's executive director.

My first day on the new job, November 1, 2007, turned out to be far more dire and onerous than I could have ever anticipated. Within my first few minutes at work, the aquarium experienced a total collapse of its computer system, initially paralyzing operations and eliminating all current and historic electronic records. Next, I discovered a file folder filled with unpaid bills totaling approximately $335,000, each representing an upset stakeholder and reflective of the poor state of the aquarium's credit-standing at that time. And then there was the state of the building and exhibits themselves. I knew going into the job that there were problems with some of the exhibits but had no idea how extensive and multi-faceted the problems were.

Our first focus was to keep the business running. We moved our email system off site and used a small email server we had in the building to run the cash registers and perform our accounting functions until a major new server could be secured and installed. Next, we contacted all the organizations to whom we owed money to assure them we intended to honor all commitments and agree to strategies for catching up on our arrears. I then asked Andy Citarella, the aquarium's IT specialist and exhibits technician, to take an inventory of the troubled exhibits and make me a list we could use as a guide in getting everything in good working order.

The list had seventeen major exhibits which were either broken or in significant disrepair. Some, like the "Great Lakes Water Table," had several major components that each needed to be individually fixed for the whole exhibit to function properly, which meant the actual number of items in need of repair was much larger than seventeen, and all very expensive. To make our focus clear to all stakeholders, we labeled our new exhibit policy, "The Three R's," which committed us to "Repair, Replace or Remove" all broken exhibits within the first six months of 2008.

Ultimately, these efforts have contributed to a remarkable, successful turnaround for the aquarium that is evident by any number of measurements.

While those efforts were underway, we turned our focus on the rest of the building by recruiting the UMD Fine Arts Department to undertake a wayfinding exercise focused on assessing signage, graphics and the overall aesthetic appeal of the facility. Three groups of senior-class fine-arts students came back with their insights and recommendations at the end of May. The plans they developed called for color-coding various exhibit areas, identifying the areas with colorful banners, creating simplified and uniform exhibit signage and developing a visitor guide to help aquarium guests more easily find their way through the facility. We liked what we saw and hired two of the students to implement their recommendations.

By early summer 2008, we had made sufficient progress on all fronts to begin looking forward to adding something new to the facility. We were eager to add an interesting selection of colorful tropical fish to our freshwater menagerie. So, we developed a new exhibit

Clockwise, starting at top left:
(1.) "The Amazing Amazon" was the first new project to be developed by the turnaround team and served as a model for all the new projects which were to follow;
(2.) Every year a new banner graced the front of the aquarium highlighting that year's featured new exhibit;
(3.) In 2015, "Shipwrecks Alive!" received a major award for "Best Interior Exhibit Design" in a national competition from the National Association for Interpretation;
(4.) Ribbon cuttings became a regular occurrence as $2.7 million in new investments in the aquarium completely transformed the facility. *(from left)* Sarah Erickson, Jay Walker, Sen. Yvonne Prettner Solon, Jack LaVoy, Naomi Yaeger, Elaine Hansen and Betty Ramsland.

gallery focused on the "Amazing Amazon," an exhibit we conceived, designed and built ourselves on a shoestring budget. This exercise served as a model for all the new projects which were to follow.

As we confronted each opportunity and assessed our options before proceeding with a new project, we would coalesce as a design team consisting of myself; Jay Walker, our director of operations; Sarah Erickson, our education director; and Bill Alworth, our finance director. We would consider the space available, the proposed theme for the exhibit, what animals might be potential candidate residents, what important lessons could be presented to the public, what we could afford to do and how we would pay for it.

From time to time, we would draw upon a group of trusted collaborators consisting of Ted Dubina, an aquarium maintenance technician who had a gift for creative carpentry and cement sculpting; Ann Gumpper, a masterful muralist and visionary set designer; Chani Becker, a highly creative and talented freelance graphics artist; Gordon Manary, a gifted artisan with a unique set of modelling and artistic carpentry skills; and Gary Nelson, a freelance master carpenter with a knack for perfection.

In 2009, we built "Freshwater Forest;" in 2010, "Masters of Disguise" and "Global Connections;" in 2011, "Aquatic Invaders" and the "Immersion Wall;" in 2012, "Fire, Ice and Rise of Life;" in 2013, "Shipwrecks Alive!;" in 2014, the "Discovery Center;" and in 2015, "Unsalted Seas," which opened the following summer. These projects represented over \$2.7 million in new investments in the aquarium and completely transformed the facility, but had we not done the work ourselves, they would have cost at least three times that amount, which would have put the transformation beyond our reach.

As we immersed ourselves in each new project, year after year, our work as a team became smoother and more cohesive as we each delved into our individual roles as part of the team. And, over time, the quality of our work continued to improve. Our faith in our efforts was finally validated when, in 2015, the National Association for Interpretation gave our "Shipwrecks Alive!" exhibit its second place "Award for Best Interior Exhibit Design," in a nationwide

Great Lakes Aquarium

The transformation of an underutilized catering kitchen and lunch room into the "Discovery Center" doubled the space available for education activities in the building and created an attractive venue for large scale meetings, receptions, and special events with a striking view of the Duluth harbor.

competition with museums and national and state parks from around the country.

During this same time, we also focused much effort upon growing the aquarium's education program, which is a function central to our core mission of promoting freshwater environmental education. Starting with three educators at the beginning of 2008, we have grown the program, under Sarah Erickson's capable leadership, to a current level of eight full-time educators and eight part-time exhibit interpreters, while doubling the space available for educational activities with the development of the "Discovery Center" in 2014, consisting of three fully-equipped classrooms and a teacher resource center.

Ultimately, these efforts have contributed to a remarkable, successful turnaround for the aquarium that is evident by any number of measurements. Since 2008, revenues and memberships have more than doubled; attendance has increased by more than 50 percent, setting successively new high levels in each of several recent years edging ever closer to the last landmark year of 2003; and the facility is debt free, with good credit, and on a sustainable operational basis, finally achieving the dream of its early visionaries and leaders.

A success story of this type could not have happened without many key contributors.

Chief among them were the incredibly talented members of our management team: Jay Walker, Sarah Erickson and Bill Alworth. The marriage of Bill's effective cash management skills with Jay and Sarah's creativity and can-do spirit made every good idea a possibility, and each of our best ideas a reality. They were absolutely invaluable to everything we achieved.

Then there were the many talented and dedicated aquarium employees who not only did outstanding work on a day-to-day basis, but when necessity called, would put in a full day's work at their regular jobs, and then spend evenings and weekends sculpting concrete, helping with carpentry, painting and any number of other tasks needed to complete a project and bring it in on time, over and over, year after year.

Additionally, the Great Lakes Aquarium board of directors, which changed and evolved over the years, played a vital role of providing strong support, guidance and encouragement, with individual members bringing a variety of valued skills and perspectives to our efforts. I want to especially acknowledge the very engaged and effective role former board chair, John Scott, played in our efforts to raise nearly $500,000, primarily from the private sector, to fund construction of the "Discovery Center."

Other important supporters include: Duluth attorney, key advisor and steadfast champion, Harold Frederick; Duluth businessman, valued counsellor and generous patron, Monnie Goldfine, and Monnie's children, Ken, Andy and Ellen; Ruth Ann Eaton and the Donald M. Weesner Foundation; Joan Gardner Goodno and the Lloyd K. Johnson Foundation; and Minnesota Power, whose MP Foundation provided an incredible $125,000 to jumpstart funding for the "Discovery Center" and whose Green Energy program partnered with the aquarium to help us save thousands of dollars per year through targeted energy conservation investments.

Since I had not been involved with the aquarium during its early years, I drew upon some key early leaders of the aquarium for support as well: Arend Sandbulte, Donn Larson, and John Anderson helped me bridge my lack of institutional knowledge and to serve as a sounding board for new ideas as they evolved. Their support was especially critical early on.

And, finally, a supportive political environment was an absolutely invaluable key to the aquarium's success as well, thanks to strong and solid support from mayors Don Ness and Emily Larson, members of the Duluth City Council and Rep. Mary Murphy and the members of the Duluth Legislative Delegation.

Together we took a struggling facility and with limited resources, a vision, and a will to make it happen, transformed Great Lakes Aquarium into a strong, sustainable institution, valued as a premier destination and Duluth's number-one paid visitor attraction. ∎

Jack LaVoy is a native of Cloquet who graduated from UMD and served in the Minnesota House of Representatives, 1971-1975. He directed several local and regional economic development organizations, then devoted 11 years as a vice president of Lake Superior Paper Industries. LaVoy was the executive director of Great Lakes Aquarium from November 2007, until his retirement in August 2018. In 1986, LaVoy was named "Business Leader of the Year" for his role in bringing a major paper mill project to Duluth, and, in 2010, he received a Lifetime Entrepreneurial Achievement Award from the UMD Labovitz School of Business and Economics. He and his wife, Nancy, live at Pike Lake and have three daughters and ten grandchildren, all of whom live in Duluth.

CHAPTER

22

Sacred Heart Music Center

A SECOND CENTURY OF SPLENDOR

by Hans Aas and Arno Kahn

Never doubt that a small group of thoughtful, committed citizens can change the world; indeed it's the only thing that ever has."
—Margaret Mead

Sacred Heart's steeple on the hill has been a Duluth landmark since 1894. In 1985 Sacred Heart Cathedral was deconsecrated by the Catholic diocese; it was not clear what would happen to the iconic building and its rare 1898 Felgemaker (Erie, Pennsylvania) pipe organ. Its place on the National Register of Historic Places, and the organ's listing on the registry of the Organ Historical Society would not be enough to save it. The threat of demolition was real and imminent.

Joan Connolly, 50-year organist at Sacred Heart, spearheaded the initial effort to preserve both the building

Brian Barber

Sacred Heart at the corner of Second Avenue West and Fourth Street.

and the organ. Connolly, with Jean Swanson and others, created the nonprofit John Chebul Memorial Center. The Catholic diocese donated the building for $1.00, the main stipulation being that it would not be used as a church. As the decade ticked by, Joan and her board members were growing older, and the situation, desperate. Meanwhile, Michael Barone's (*Pipedreams*, Minnesota Public Radio) crucial early efforts to champion the Felgemaker had brought about an expanded awareness of this forgotten treasure.

A small group of interested Duluthians including Janet Blixt, Gail Dahlberg, Phil Bradley and David Tryggestad offered Connolly a friendly board "takeover," and in June 1994, a new board was formed; Janet Blixt was elected president. (A vote taken at a March 1994 meeting of the previous board had determined against demolition, and the retiring board welcomed a totally new effort.) The nonprofit arts organization was renamed the Sacred Heart Music Center. Short-term goals focused on the adaptive re-use of the remarkable space as a living, breathing performing arts center, with the jewel in its crown, the Felgemaker organ. The board's long-term vision was no less than to be a leader and visible symbol in the future revitalization of the Central Hillside.

1994-96 were intensely busy years. Board members joked that a prerequisite to joining the project was insanity. The aging building was in crisis. The roof and organ needed immediate repair, the steam heat cranked out excessive damp, the floor was treacherous, paint was peeling off the walls, and there were no public bathrooms. Board, advisory board, membership, volunteer and audience bases had to be built. The early musical programming meant all hands on deck: board and advisory board members cleaned, baked, hosted, performed at events. Audience members in need of a restroom were directed across the street to the Damiano Center facilities.

The first membership drive brought in 120 members. The board applied for various grants to simultaneously preserve the building and expand its musical programming: a $6,000 matching grant from the Minnesota Historical Society and funds from the Duluth Preservation Alliance funded critical initial work on the central bell tower steeple. The Arrowhead Regional Arts Council provided support to present

Felgemaker organ.

the Minneapolis Community Gospel Choir, and with a McKnight small capital grant, helped the board achieve restrooms within the building.

The initial focus of the center was classical music, but the board realized that Sacred Heart must showcase every kind of performance in its remarkable acoustic. The board from 1994 on expanded the music offerings beyond Duluth artists to regional, national and international events. Early local and regional artists included: the rock band Low with Mimi and Alan Sparhawk, Bill Bastian, Ed Martin, Tom Wegren, Zuni Migoze, Lyz Jaakola, Sara Thomsen, Charlie Parr, Haley Bonar, Robert Robinson, Keri Noble, Billy McLaughlin, Peter Mayer, SimpleGifts, Greg Brown, Arrowhead Chorale, Hermantown Youth Chorus (later the Lake Superior Youth Chorus) under direction of Jerry Kaldor and Class Ring under direction of Bill Alexander. The Sacred Heart Centennial Chorus and Orchestra under the direction of David Tryggestad (all volunteer) presented a dozen concerts from

1994 to 2003 including the Fauré *Requiem*, Mozart *Requiem*, Lauridsen *Lux Aeterna*, and Britten *Ceremony of Carols*. The list of national and international artists over the years is astonishing: Emily Van Evera, Rose Ensemble, Arlo Guthrie, Crash Test Dummies, Ladysmith Black Mambazo, jazz harpist Park Stickney, Mason Jennings, Altan, April Verch, the Beth Custer Ensemble, Spencer Myer and Erika Wueschner, Marcia Ball, Emma Kirkby, Vienna Boys Choir (twice), and the Okee Dokee Brothers.

Constant donations of time and work from Duluth organ builder Dan Jaeckel and his crew kept the organ playable through the early decades. The local American Guild of Organists (AGO) continue to present regular recitals on the Felgemaker. Local and regional players include: Norma Stevlingson, David Tryggestad, Carole Donahue, Tom Hamilton, Rachel Kresha, Jason Branham, and the late Janet MacCleod and the late John Vanella. National and international performers include: Jess Eschbach, Michael Corzine, Grethe Krogh, Christopher Bowers-Broadbent, Bruce Bengtson, and Aaron David Miller.

In the early years, the late Janet MacCleod was the organ curator, charged with day-to-day care of the organ. In recent years, David Tryggestad has been resident organist and the recently established Friends of the Felgemaker are collectively responsible for the instrument. This group, chaired by Velda Bell, raised $43,000 to hire Wahl Organ of Appleton, Wis., to remove, clean, and replace the Felgemaker pipes in the summer of 2017. The organ was gloriously ready by August 11 to host Bruce Bengtson in recital as a part of the national convention of the Organ Historical Society.

Among the creative adaptive uses for Sacred Heart has been its growing reputation as a marvelous recording space. Eric Swanson and Low recorded the center's initial non-classical CD and held their release party in September 2002 at Sacred Heart. Since then, a variety of local and national artists have made use of the studio. Tom Fabjance and Jake Larson are sound engineers who have worked with Eric Swanson in recent years.

The center has continued to expand its mission as a more inclusive community center. The Music Resource Center (MRC) introduces young people to music performance. The MRC program, operated

Brian Barber

From the balcony, set-up for an Electric Witch video with Mike Scholtz, Zac Bentz, Steph Bentz, and Greg Connolly.

by the Armory Arts Center, is held at Sacred Heart twice a week after school. Sacred Heart hosted a Democracy Now gathering in 2016 and the first annual Femn Fest in September 2017.

Available for rental, Sacred Heart is a popular site for weddings and other significant life events. In addition to its incredible musical properties, it boasts stunning stained glass windows and movable seating on gleaming maple floors.

Over the past three decades, the Sacred Heart Music Center story has been a tale of collective minds, wills, and hearts challenged by an aging structure in a difficult climate. A small army of people has lent its energies to raising funds to maintain the magical space and expand its impact. In 1999, the Splendor II capital campaign had vigorously ramped up its efforts. Funds raised over the last ten years brought the building to a physical state only dreamed of in the previous years.

Current board president, Hans Aas, has been at the helm of the efforts since January 2003, ably assisted in recent years by vice

Brian Barber

Guitarist Darin Bergsven seen rehearsing from upstage.

president, Arno Kahn. Additional key volunteers have been: Janet Blixt, Michael Barone, Mary Van Evera, John Kelly, Gene Halvorson, Max Ramsland, Barb Darland, David Schilling, Jerry Agnew, Dan King, Stephen Lewis, Maryanne Norton, Susan Maki, Lynn Tryggestad, Jill Fisher, LuAnne Anderson, Karen Ruona, Cheryl Reitan, Christobel Grant, Jess Eschbach, Beatrice Dwyer, Janet Pearson Ulleberg, Terry Anderson, Penny Perry, Tracy Schram, Joe Modec, and Sarah Parker.

Since the very beginning, Sacred Heart has undergone constant repairs and renovation. Most of these projects were overseen by Hans Aas and Arno Kahn. Local construction firms carried out the work. Noel Knudsen was the project architect, with recent help from Hugh Reitan. Dennis Hurst and Jim Berry with Hurst/Hendrichs were the structural engineers. Significant improvements to the building include: new bathrooms, new hot water heating system, plaster interior repair and painting by Len Pekkala, removal and reconstruction of the main floor, steel reinforcing added to the bell tower, removal and replacement of failed masonry, roof replacement and repair to the east annex after a truck drove through the wall.

As Sacred Heart continues to evolve, its intent is to involve an expanding base of younger members, volunteers, and musicians. The board continues to explore fundraising options and hopes to obtain a grant to fund a half-time executive director. New musicians are always added to the playlist and Friends of the Felgemaker has taken on the Second Saturday concert series and a large holiday performance. A weeklong residency is in the works, and numerous building projects await completion.

In March of 2018 Low performed a fundraiser show, opened by Ingeborg von Agassiz, for Sacred Heart, Friends of the Felgemaker, and CHUM. The band was commissioned specifically to include the Felgemaker organ. The musicians and the community made the show an amazing success and another shining moment in the rich history of the place and the organ.

Much of the Music Center's success can be attributed to the many, many individuals and organizations that have demonstrated their love and appreciation for music and history. With your valued participation, Sacred Heart Music Center will continue to flourish. ∎

Duluth News Tribune

Hans Aas and his wife Martha were among the original founding members of the Sacred Heart Music Center and have been loyal contributors since day one. Hans is a retired physician, formerly practicing at what is Essentia today.

Arno Kahn, too, has served faithfully since the Cathedral property was purchased for $1 in the '70s. Arno, a founder of Builder's Commonwealth, came equipped with construction and maintenance knowledge which has steered countless physical improvements and restoration.

CHAPTER

23

American Indian Community Housing Organization

GIMAAJII MINO-BIMAADIZIMIN
(WE ARE, ALL OF US TOGETHER, BEGINNING A GOOD LIFE)

by LeAnn Littlewolf

(Anishinaabe, Gaa-Zagaskwaajimekaag, Maa'iingan Doodem)

In the traditional origin story *of the Anishinaabeg Indigenous people, Sky Woman falls from a world above. The animals see her falling and fear for her because the world is only water. The turtle offers his back, if only someone can dive to the depths below to retrieve a handful of earth. All of the strongest attempt, but no one is successful. Finally, Washashk (muskrat) says he will try. They all doubt him because he is so small. He makes his dive anyway and all the animals wait in anticipation. He is gone for a long time and the animals think he has perished. But, barely alive, he surfaces. In his tiny paw, he clenches a handful of earth. They quickly place the earth on turtle's back and it becomes the world we now know, with trees, plants and everything we need to sustain ourselves. It becomes home for Sky Woman and her children, the Anishinaabeg.*

Karen Savage-Blue

(above) Creation by Karen Savage-Blue.

(right) AICHO's new solar panel array on the AICHO garden rooftop, with the first large scale Indigenous public art mural painted by the Indigenous artist collective NSRGNTS. AICHO is the first low-income housing complex in the nation to have a solar rooftop array on an urban Indian Center.

Photo by Ivy Vainio

Like Washashk when he arrives with the earth in his hand, AICHO (American Indian Community Housing Organization) is bringing new ground for our people.

AN ORIGIN STORY

The origin story of AICHO starts in a parking lot outside a local social service agency with a conversation between Native community members who asked why our community had no resources, no community spaces, and no services that met our cultural needs. In 1993, AICHO was created as an Indigenous response to social conditions in Duluth, powered by the urban Native American community.

AICHO started with basic needs — shelter, housing, support — and has grown to work toward changing systems to offset the impact of violence, housing and economic inequity, historical trauma and racism. AICHO provides a continuum of community action, housing options, and support services. We started with nothing. Today, we offer an American Indian community center, 44 units of permanent supportive housing, a domestic violence emergency shelter, legal advocacy, youth programming, a newly launched social enterprise program, and initiatives in climate and cultural resiliency, food sovereignty, and arts and culture.

All of our work is anchored in our mission, which is to honor the resiliency of Indigenous people by strengthening communities and centering Indigenous values in all aspects of our work. Our philosophy is that every American Indian person deserves to live in a non-violent and non-threatening environment and has the right to be treated with dignity and respect.

LAND-BASED ECONOMY AND ECONOMIC JUSTICE

To understand the significance of AICHO, the historical context is necessary. Duluth is in the heart of Indigenous territory that was ceded, and it holds strong spiritual and cultural significance to our people. Many American Indians relocate to Duluth for education or employment opportunities, and some seek sobriety support in a new environment. The federal policies of the relocation era also played a role in driving Indigenous people to urban areas. Traditional land-based economy provided a dynamic food system, homes, clothing, goods, transportation and medicine — everything necessary for communities to thrive. The Ojibwe people lost more than land in the treaty process. This economic context is what drives AICHO to reclaim cultural practices, traditional ties to the land, and rebirth of Indigenous economic health.

The land ceded in the treaty process built immense wealth for others, including the agricultural, timber, mining, and shipping industries that propelled Minnesota to economic prosperity. But today, the Indigenous community in Duluth is at ground zero in terms of poverty. Nearly 65 percent of Native Americans in Duluth are living at or below the poverty level, compared to 22 percent of the overall population (2013 American Community Survey). Native Americans comprise less than 3 percent of the city population and yet represent more than 30 percent in the Duluth homeless count (Wilder Study 2003).

Indigenous women, who traditionally held key economic and decision-making positions, were hit hard by colonization and new gender norms that unbalanced community power. These changes weakened overall economic and community viability. In Minnesota, 80 percent of American Indian mothers are the primary breadwinners in families (compared to 46 percent of white mothers), yet 37.1 percent of American Indian women live in poverty, the highest poverty rate of all races (Status of Women and Girls in Minnesota, 2014). What happens to Indigenous women directly impacts the economic well-being of the family, and disruptions ripple out into the community.

NEW GROUND-GIMAAJII MINO-BIMAADIZIMIN

In 2007, AICHO embarked on a journey to reclaim a place of our own in Duluth. AICHO purchased the historic YWCA building located in downtown Duluth. For five years, AICHO worked to raise funds and build partnerships to create a dynamic mixed-use space and maximize the 50,000-square-foot building's capacity using a strategy known as creative placemaking, or building a community in which a core of arts, culture and creativity drives prosperity and growth. After raising over $8 million from a variety of federal, state, local and private sources, AICHO moved forward with its creative, intentional design, including on-site permanent supportive housing; interspersed leased offices for Tribal organizations; community and resident spaces in the Robert Powless Cultural Center (formerly known as Trepanier Hall*); meeting rooms; a gymnasium; a commercial kitchen; supportive services; a social enterprise business, Indigenous First Art & Gift Shop; and the urban rooftop garden with a newly installed solar panel array. The building is called Gimaajii.

Gimaajii provides access to housing, economic opportunities, arts and cultural events and supportive programming. Support groups, talking circles, Indigenous language instruction, and cultural activities fill the building every week. Community members attend events at Gimaajii, from traditional feasts and ceremonies to community forums and AICHO's arts and cultural events. Gimaajii creates space to articulate needs and share ideas on moving the community forward.

CREATIVE PARTNERSHIPS

From the beginning, AICHO developed meaningful partnerships with Tribal Nations to leverage resources. For instance, AICHO and its partners have established subsidized apartments, mental health services that generate higher third-party billing rates, and Tribal band member access to resources (White Earth Nation Mental Health, Leech Lake Nation Urban office, Fond du Lac housing access).

Gimaajii's central, prominent location showcases the first large-scale Indigenous public art piece in Duluth: a mural created collaboratively by AICHO, Honor the Earth, and the artist group NSRGNTS, to bring attention to water rights and water protectors, missing and murdered Indigenous women, and the presence of Indigenous people and our ties to this land. The community joined in painting mural sections, fundraising, and celebrating the finished image. At the unveiling event, over 500 community members participated in a healing and drum ceremony, artist presentation, and

---

*Named in honor of the family of Lois Trepanier Paulucci.

Photo by Ivy Vainio

Traditional Asemaa (sacred tobacco) teaching with Nikki Crowe and Gimaajii families.

traditional feast. The mural image has since gone international and symbolizes a call to action.

In 2012, AICHO developed urban rooftop gardens with no direct funding. By 2017, AICHO had developed its Climate and Cultural Resilience (CCR) initiative, which became one of only five programs nationally to receive funding from Enterprise Community Partners, Inc. AICHO created the CCR Advisory Council, comprised of Gimaajii residents, Native community members, elders and AICHO staff to guide the initiative. The CCR initiative has brought about the addition of a 12-KW grid-tied roof solar array, expansion of the rooftop garden space, a new water collection system, and large-scale worm composting. This past winter, AICHO partnered with Duluth Area Chamber of Commerce's Leadership Duluth (community business leaders) volunteer group to design and build the new rooftop garden. The Leadership Duluth group brought engineering, architectural, and monetary resources to the project, including donated labor. Leadership Duluth and the CCR Advisory Council worked together to develop focus on traditional ecological knowledge and ways to keep costs down while building long-term sustainability. This cross-cultural collaboration drives our progress forward.

CULTURAL COMMUNITY STRATEGIES

To be community-driven, community must be present. AICHO hosts more than 500 community events every year and welcomes more than 11,000 individual guests every year. These events create opportunities for intergenerational and cross-cultural connections. AICHO events feature dynamic variety: art shows that highlight contemporary Indigenous themes; traditional feasts and ceremonies; music concerts; Indigenous films; and honoring ceremonies. The art and culture initiative has generated recognition of AICHO's resourcefulness and ingenuity.

AICHO is rebuilding community and cultural health through a vibrant Indigenous art movement. AICHO renamed Trepanier Hall, a larger meeting hall with a stage, as the Dr. Robert Powless Cultural Center, named after a highly respected American Indian community elder. The Dr. Robert Powless Cultural Center hosts over 300 community, cultural, and arts events per year. AICHO has developed staff positions to advertise and promote art events, set up and organize events, and build an informal network of Indigenous artists.

Two community spaces at Gimaajii were converted to Indigenous art galleries and feature local and regional Indigenous visual artists. Indigenous First Art & Gift Shop opened in 2017 and features 77 different artists. In 2018, AICHO secured funding to initiate a small revolving loan program for emerging artists to obtain materials or fund other production costs for art-related business endeavors. The Indigenous First Art & Gift Shop has been in operation for nine months, with outstanding success.

AICHO helps our community reclaim traditional foods and make fresh food more accessible. Guided by food sovereignty principles, AICHO builds health through Indigenous food practices (traditional growing, gathering, harvesting), ceremonies and traditional feasts onsite, and consistent cultural teachings and support groups. Our big dream for the future is a new Indigenous economy in Duluth — a robust Indigenous strand to a strong local economy. Like a sweetgrass braid, the three strands — Indigenous housing, arts and culture, and food — create this new economy.

Building on the success of Indigenous First Art & Gift Shop, AICHO plans to expand its business offerings. Projects currently in the works include an Indigenous food market, where Native food producers can showcase traditional foods, and a deli/cafe featuring Indigenous recipes; a stand-alone coffee shop in Lincoln Park with performance venue and art retail space; micro-businesses focused on healthy, local food; and an art frame shop.

AICHO's story reaches back into the roots of a traditional perspective that tells us to dive deep for our people and bring up new things that will sustain us far into the future — and our story is rooted in the deep relationships within our community. ∎

LeAnn Littlewolf (Anishinaabe, Gaa-Zagaskwaajimekaag, Maa'iingan Doodem) is on a leadership team at AICHO for a food sovereignty initiative and development of Indigenous social enterprises, and assists with program/ initiative development. LeAnn has worked in the nonprofit and policy advocacy sectors for more than 25 years, which includes direct services, development, and executive director roles, and carries a deep commitment to community leadership. She holds a master's degree in education and a master's degree in advocacy and political leadership.

AUTHOR ACKNOWLEDGMENTS

AICHO's Partners for the Rooftop Project & Urban Gardens.

Minnesota Interfaith Power & Light

Whole Foods Co-op

Duluth Area Chamber of Commerce's Leadership Duluth

Climate & Cultural Resiliency Advisory Council

Ecolibrium3

Rural Reliable Energy Alliance (RREAL)

Minnesota Power Solar Sense

Ordean Foundation

Lloyd K. Johnson Foundation

Notah Begay III Foundation

Northland Foundation

First Nations Development Institute

Individual contributions from many community members

St. Peter's Church

VISION AND DEDICATION
CREATE A FINE ARTS ACADEMY FOR DULUTH

by Jeffrey T. Larson

We'd spent days driving around Duluth looking for the perfect building to house our dream. Our hopes were high; our standards, higher. The building would have to be relatively large, at least 4,000 square feet. Tall ceilings, a must. And most importantly, plenty north-facing windows.

It was August 2015. One week prior to our building search, my wife Heidi and I had invited our friend, the accomplished Patricia Burns, and then-City-Councilor Emily Larson to my art studio to present our dream of opening a classical fine arts academy in Duluth. Heidi and I and our son, Brock, had been talking about it for several years. Brock had recently graduated from a five-year study at the same fine arts atelier that I had graduated from 30 years earlier.

In 1980, at the age of 17, I was blessedly accepted into the full-time program at Atelier Lack in Minneapolis.

Jeffrey T. Larson

St. Peter's Church at 818 West Third Street.

Founded by Richard Lack, it was one of fewer than a dozen schools in the world, to the best of my awareness, still passing on a 500-year accumulative knowledge of Western art-picture-making. Through the end of the nineteenth century, this training had continually developed and improved. Then the advent of modernist philosophy deemed this approach to art-teaching unnecessary, and even harmful, to creativity. By the mid-20th century, much of this knowledge had been nearly lost. Our dream was to build a classical training program for modern artists and keep the knowledge of Western art-picture-making growing.

Patricia and Emily believed in our mission and encouraged us to move forward. So the following week, there we were, driving around the city in search of a place upon which to reflect our vision. Except nothing was fitting the bill. Then a friend asked us, "What about the old St. Peter's Church?"

I had never heard of it. We went to take a look. It was a vacant, boarded-up, stone church, old and appearing neglected. It was also large with tall ceilings and plenty north-facing windows.

Completed in 1926, St. Peter's Church was built by the Italian congregants, many of whom skilled stone masons and brick layers who also built Enger Tower and the Seven Bridges, among countless other buildings and homes in Duluth. The church quickly became the vibrant center of Duluth's "Little Italy," a community comprised largely of the city's Italian immigrants. The church remained a neighborhood hub for decades, abuzz with activity daily, before sunup and past sundown. Over time, and unfortunately in line with a broader trend, shrinking congregational membership forced the diocese to close the church. 2010 marked the last service at St. Peter's Church.

By the time we came upon it, the church had been vacant with no heat or electricity for several years. Battles to save the building had been waged, but it seemed to be heading toward demolition. One publication had listed St. Peter's Church as one of the five most important endangered historic buildings in Minnesota. It was advertised that the clay tile roof needed to be replaced, and that it had shifted off its foundation, among many other pitfalls and problems. Rich with local history, and a longstanding symbol of fellowship and community, the St. Peter's Church building hung in the balance.

We saw the potential to bring our dream to life in that old church. We decided to take a gamble. And in November 2015, we won the bid and closed the sale just one day before the diocese declared bankruptcy, which would have potentially tied the building up in a legal hold for years.

The following January, with help from family and friends (and with no heat or running water), we began deconstructing the inside of the church. After filling three dumpsters, I decided to order the fourth one at half-size, thinking we must be close to finished. We ended up filling a total of 16 dumpsters by the time the project was finished — an early and lasting lesson on a steep learning curve.

It would be 18 months of 12-hour days, including weekends, of solid work for my family and a multitude of carpenters, electricians,

Jeffrey T. Larson

(Above and right) Artists at work in the renovated church's studio space.

plumbers, masons, plasterers, heating specialists, insulators, etc. to completely gut and renovate the building. We tore everything out, back to the bare walls, and started over: new electrical, plumbing, heating, and HVAC. We kept as much of the old building showing as we could, converting it into a modern facility to meet a new set of needs. It had also, to our pleasant surprise, not shifted a bit on its foundation, which was bedrock. And that roof that needed replacement only cost us $600 in materials to repair.

Dismantling walls elevated our vision. The Great Lakes Academy of Fine Art was taking shape. Inspired by Atelier Lack, alma mater to my son and me, we imagined our own school rising up in this revived church and reveled in the possibility of building on an opulent history of art-teaching and art-making.

Richard Lack, the aforementioned founder of Atelier Lack, had studied in Boston with Ives Gammell, who had studied with William M. Paxton (one of the Boston Ten), who had studied with Gerome

Jeffrey T. Larson

in Paris in the 1800s. Gerome had studied with Deleroche, who had studied with Ingres, who had studied with David (both of whom painted Nepoleon). The glorious history of Western art is primarily predicated upon the passing on of the growing accumulated knowledge and skills as practiced by each generation of painters. Each century is punctuated by the geniuses whose work we see in museums and art history books, yet their work would be nothing without the training that they had received as young students. This training is the knowledge that was nearly lost, and its teaching exists in few places. The Great Lakes Academy of Fine Art (GLAFA) is one of only a small number of art schools in the world that is passing on the craftsmanship of oil painting as taught in the late nineteenth century Paris ateliers.

We thought we'd wait to find students until building renovation was complete, but students found us first. We accepted six students early on, and they began studying in the fall of 2016 in an unfinished space and less than optimal conditions. It's testimony to a classical style revival and an inspired vision coming together in a promising, treasured building.

Those beautiful church windows let in light from the north, indirect light ideal for art spaces because it limits the shadow play caused by direct sunlight. The main sanctuary is the primary working studio for the full-time students. We added a cast room with controlled light for beginners. This is where first-year students learn the fundamentals of shapes, values, and light transitions (edges) working from plaster casts of famous sculptures. Downstairs on the first floor, we have room set aside for the part-time program (teaching the same information on a part-time schedule). On off time, the space can house seminars. We also have a rental studio designed for graduate students to work in after they have completed their studies, in their transition from student to professional fine artist. There is a common full kitchen and dining lounge, plus an apartment suitable for a couple of live-in students. Brock and I plan to each have our own studios, and we plan to add a small frame shop and etching press area.

GLAFA is structured as a four-year apprenticeship. The full-time program consists of up to 16 dedicated aspiring professional fine artists. Much as a serious musician must not only learn how to play their instrument, but master it, an artist who is in love with the beauty of the visual world must study and master the fundamentals of the painters craft before they too can blossom into their full potential. Our goal is to train modern artists to paint at a level primarily seen in museums and to contribute our passion for fine art toward today's practice. Painting our dream onto the virtual legacy-mural of the old St. Peter's Church is an added blessing. ∎

Jeffrey T. Larson was born in 1962 in Two Harbors, MN and grew up in the Twin Cities. Jeffrey has been trained in the manner of the Old Masters at the prestigious Atelier Lack, a studio/school whose traditions and training methods reach back through impressionism and the 19th century's French academies. He followed his four-year formal training with museum study in the United States and abroad and has now opened his own atelier, Great Lakes Academy of Fine Art in Duluth.

PUBLIC BUILDINGS

"We shape our buildings;
thereafter they shape us."

—Winston Churchill, from a 1943 debate

CHAPTER

25

Duluth International Airport

UPGRADING OUR REGION'S FRONT DOOR

by Brian Ryks

As the front door to the region, the Duluth International Airport connects the Northland to the rest of the world. Competitive air service is pivotal to Duluth-Superior's long-term vitality, supporting its business attraction and retention, tourism, and overall economic health.

The Duluth Airport Authority and its seven-member board of directors supports day-to-day operation and annual capital improvements without collecting a general tax levy — a testament to its business-oriented leadership and historic values. Major tenants of the Duluth International Airport include the 148th Fighter Wing, Cirrus Design, Monaco Air Duluth, and AAR, who collectively provide over 2,000 jobs locally and generate over $1.9 billion in annual economic impact.

Courtesy of RS&H, Inc.

Old Duluth Airport terminal.

The post-9-11 Department of Homeland Security and the Transportation Security Administration (TSA) ushered in a new era of air travel. The layout of the 40-year-old Duluth International Airport terminal building posed significant challenges. Equipment necessary to carry out new security protocols and meet technology requirements forced airline passengers into small secure glass-enclosed rooms with limited seating and no concessions or restrooms. The environment no longer lent itself to an exceptional travel experience, let alone long-term growth of air service in the Twin Ports. In fact, it had become unacceptable.

I recall my first observation upon arriving as airport manager in 2002: the airport needed major renovations in multiple areas of the terminal complex. I stepped out onto a parking lot, which was in dire shape, a rusty guardrail separating short-term from long-term parking. Rental car storage forced passengers to the furthest corner of the lot, which meant trudging through drifting snow on cold winter evenings. A small single elevator ran from the lower level up to passenger ticketing, baggage claim, and boarding levels. Leaky, stained skylights shed minimal natural light into the dark facility, adorned with antiquated finishes. The cobblestone tile floor designed prior to the rise of roller bags met the plastic luggage wheels with a loud chatter. And outside on the runway, aircraft tails penetrated critical Federal Aviation Administration (FAA) protection zones during passenger loading, a safety violation borne by FAA regulation updates since the airport's 1963 construction.

Shortly after my arrival, the Airport Board approved the concept of facility improvement, and we engaged architects to determine the best path forward. Our first approach, an estimated $45-million remodel of the existing facility, left many uncertainties and still wouldn't solve the FAA protection zone problem. During our discussion and deliberation of a major facility overhaul, a change in the political environment redirected our conversation. The late Congressman Jim Oberstar, long-time representative of District 8 and aviation advocate, was appointed chairman of the powerful House of Representatives Transportation and Infrastructure Committee, producing what the board saw as a once-in-a-lifetime opportunity.

The board reconvened and decided to pursue the potential of constructing a new facility in light of the newfound possibility of elevated federal support. We developed four concepts and locations. The least expensive option involved constructing the new facility in the existing main terminal parking lot, and then demolishing the existing facility once the new terminal was available for occupancy. A challenging proposition! A four-year multi-phase construction project wouldn't easily accommodate passengers moving through the existing facility. Not to mention the task of developing a finance plan for an estimated $80 million project. But a new terminal, a new front door for the Duluth-Superior region, would serve the Northland for many years. And we were determined to accomplish this goal without the requirement of local taxpayer dollars.

The project would not succeed without the support of the City of Duluth and the area business community. We'd have to justify the need in order to move forward. Justifying the need posed an interesting conundrum: we needed to improve the facility to accommodate growth; and we needed to show growth in order to win support for facility improvements.

In order to grow our passenger volume at our current facility, we needed to expand upon the five or six daily flights to Minneapolis. Investment in air service development became a priority. The first big success: Northwest Airlines added non-stop service from Duluth to their Detroit hub. Shortly thereafter we landed Allegiant Air, an ultra-low-cost carrier providing service to Las Vegas. Allegiant Air's low fares stimulated the market, and soon customers were coming from as far away as Thunder Bay to take advantage of their non-stop service to a warm destination. Allegiant's 150-passenger MD80 aircraft put further demand on the airport's passenger screening system and passenger hold rooms, all designed for lesser capacity. This demand highlighted the need for upgrades. The business community began to notice the increased activity and the desire to improve the customer experience.

During this time, I became involved in a private sector initiative to establish a regional economic development organization focused on retaining existing jobs and bringing new business opportunities to the area. The Airport Authority became a founding member of the Area Partnership for Expansion, known as APEX. Rob West, APEX's then-CEO, understood the importance of air service in retaining and attracting business to the Twin Port's region and became a partner in our goal to build a new terminal. APEX was also the conduit for connecting the airport with leadership of the area's largest businesses.

We needed the business community's assistance in moving the new terminal initiative forward. We sought input from businesses to weigh the options: a $45-million remodel of the existing terminal, or a completely new terminal at a price tag of $80 million. The response overwhelmingly pointed to building new. This provided us justification to pursue federal funding. We met with Congressman Oberstar, who pledged his support. Next stop, obtaining buy-in from the State Office of Aeronautics in St. Paul and the FAA Airports District Office in Minneapolis. Then it would be on to FAA Headquarters in Washington. Numerous meetings ensued with each agency. At the same time, we continued to expand air service at the Duluth International Airport. Allegiant added service to Phoenix and Orlando, and we landed United Airlines to Chicago. With each new air service addition, we set passenger records at the airport, growing support and momentum as we went.

While the State Office of Aeronautics and FAA agreed the project was justified, they wanted proof that we had a solid financial plan prior to pledging the first state and federal dollars. Our plan was to maximize federal funding and then fill the gap with a combination of State Aeronautics dollars, Duluth Airport Authority revenue, TSA grants, customer and passenger revenue, and finally something that had never been accomplished previously for a Minnesota airport terminal project, state bonding dollars.

The most significant challenge would be selling the project to the Minnesota State Legislature. Senators Tom Bakk and Yvonne Prettner Solon authored and championed the project with strong support from representatives Tom Huntley, Mary Murphy, and Roger Reinert. After numerous meetings with the majority of committee members over the course of two years as the House and Senate bills proceeded through committees, and tireless project promotion at "Duluth and St. Louis County Days at the Capitol," the project garnered $4.9 million of support in 2009 and another $11.7 million in 2010. Our financial plan was now complete, consisting of 12 different funding sources, none of which requiring direct local taxpayer dollars.

I thought we'd crossed the biggest hurdle. Little did I know, we would begin construction during the most challenging Federal Airport Improvement Funding cycle to date. Typically, Congress passes an FAA reauthorization bill for a multi-year period, which allows airports to maintain a consistent and stable funding source for projects that are phased over a period of time. We thought our four-year construction timing was perfect. What we didn't know is that the House and Senate would be unable to agree on a long-term aviation bill, and as a result, issue short-term extensions to the existing bill. This limited the FAA's ability to issue previously committed grants for the project. In other words, we'd be forced to bid multiple individual phases of the project without assurance the federal grant dollars would be received to award the work.

Meanwhile, under the new Obama administration, an opportunity brewed as Congress began discussing a possible stimulus package for shovel-ready projects. Once I heard this, I instructed our engineers to fast track the first phase design to position us for a potential stimulus application. Our engineering team worked expeditiously to design the inbound roadway and new parking lot

The new DLH boasts a laidback experience with little to no waiting at check-in and security.

as I worked with Congressman Oberstar and the FAA to ensure the project could compete nationally. Shortly thereafter, the stimulus (ARRA) program became a reality, and in 2009, we received our first funding of $5 million to commence the project. The next four years brought a flurry of construction activity — designing, bidding, awarding contracts — sensitive to minimizing travelers' disruption through each phase. Ongoing federal funding uncertainty prompted numerous visits to FAA headquarters in Washington and with our congressional delegation to keep the project at top-of-mind amongst our federal and state delegates.

Countless people rallied for the project, and in January 2013 the community celebrated, in a flurry of fanfare, the grand opening of the Duluth International Airport terminal, a true community accomplishment.

The new terminal accommodates efficient movement by separating inbound from outbound passenger flows. A versatile customs and border protection facility allows passenger waiting and baggage claim areas to convert between international and domestic flights for maximum efficiency. An inline baggage inspection system, funded by the TSA, eliminates the manual searching of bags. We were the first airport in Minnesota to apply for and receive the Voluntary Airport Low Emissions (VALE) federal grant, which we used to install a geothermal heating and cooling system and aircraft gate electrification, replacing diesel fueled auxiliary power units with electric plug-ins. These changes save the airport and airlines millions of dollars each year and reduce carbon gas emissions.

From an aesthetic standpoint, modern designs incorporate the heritage of the Twin Ports. The curved roof represents a wave on Lake Superior. The reddish-rust tint of the outside building panels were chosen to reflect the William Irvin iron-ore ship docked in Canal Park. Plenty of exterior glass promotes natural light throughout the facility.

Upon completion, the entire project included 11 different FAA Airport Improvement Program and TSA grants totaling $47 million — more federal grant dollars than any other terminal building of its size. State bonding dollars of $16.6 million demonstrated to the FAA that we had the required matching funds to leverage the federal dollars. Other grants of $5 million from the Minnesota State Office of Aeronautics, $2.4 million from the TSA, and $7.6 million in passenger and customer facility charges. A remaining $1.4 million in cash from the Duluth Airport Authority completed the project without any direct local taxpayer dollars.

The new Duluth International Airport terminal plays a critical role in regional business expansion and new business opportunities by offering quality air service and the amenities passengers have become accustomed to in an airport. The investment in this state-of-the-art facility, connecting Duluth to the rest of the world, provides a modern front door reflecting a prosperous region and a strong economy. This impression will serve the region well and have a lasting impression on everyone who passes through it. ∎

Brian D. Ryks, A.A.E. was appointed executive director and CEO of the Metropolitan Airports Commission in May 2016. He is responsible for the administration and management of Minneapolis St. Paul International Airport and the MAC's six reliever airports. Before arriving in Minneapolis, he held a similar positions as executive director and CEO of the Gerald R. Ford International Airport in Grand Rapids, Michigan from 2012-2016, executive director of the Duluth Airport Authority from 2002-2012, airport manager at the St. Cloud Regional Airport from 1997-2002, airport manager at the Aberdeen Regional Airport, SD from 1996-1997 and manager of noise abatement at Stapleton and Denver International Airports from 1990-1996. He began his career as a noise technician at the Metropolitan Airports Commission in 1986.

CHAPTER

26

AMSOIL Arena

A SYMBOL OF COMMUNITY CONFIDENCE

by Dan Russell

The March 10, 2000 headline on the front page of the *Duluth News Tribune* read, "UMD eyes an on campus facility for Men's Hockey." The time had come for a new, modern arena for the UMD hockey teams.

As UMD looked at the potential to house a new arena on campus, the DECC Board of Directors committed to maintaining its long relationship with UMD Hockey, its largest tenant. The Duluth business community recognized the tremendous economic impact an arena has on a downtown. The question became, where would the new arena go?

Influential leaders involved in the original Duluth Arena/Auditorium — such as Judge Gerald Heaney, Erv and Monnie Goldfine, and Jeno Paulucci — weighed in, favoring UMD Hockey be kept at the DECC. But everyone involved also realized it was time to start planning

Bob Horn

Five months after groundbreaking. Construction site as viewed from Symphony Hall.

Bob Horn

Construction site seven months after groundbreaking. Concrete stadia and steel beams.

for a new arena, a facility that would include a larger NHL-sized ice sheet, suites, and a modern scoreboard and player facilities. The DECC Board hired a local architectural firm, Stanius Johnson, who partnered with the world's largest venue designer, HOK (now Populous), to develop a preliminary design and cost estimates.

The DECC Board worked with the City of Duluth to develop a financing plan to pay for the proposed $80-million arena. The final plan called for a request of $40 million in bonding money from the State of Minnesota, matched by a $40-million contribution from the City of Duluth. The City's bond payments would comprise DECC revenue, UMD rent, and a new .75% food and beverage sales tax.

There was tremendous competition at the time for state bonding support for sports venues. The University of Minnesota's Twin Cities branch had plans for a new football stadium; the Minnesota Twins wanted support for a new field; and the Minnesota Vikings were in the middle of their longtime quest for a new stadium.

Governor Tim Pawlenty strongly believed there should be local referendums for each of these projects and excluded them in his 2006 bonding proposal. He committed his support of Duluth's proposed arena with a caveat: Duluthians get the chance to vote on the new sales tax to fund the project.

The City of Duluth answered the governor's challenge and scheduled a special referendum.

"Arena Yes" formed to advocate for building a new arena; community leaders, George Downs and Darlene Marshall co-chaired, and local public relations expert, Steve Greenfield, coordinated the campaign. Duluth businesses donated a combined $40,000 toward the effort. The community faced a huge choice.

In some ways, the choice faced by the community felt more significant than whether or not to build a new arena. Underlying the nuts-and-bolts questions of taxes and expenditures was a larger question about the level of optimism and confidence in Duluth's future. It was a question of the level of ambition that Duluthians had for their city. Were we resigned to the rust-belt narrative that encouraged us to simply manage our decline, or were we willing to take a bold, some would say risky, bet on our own future?

Dan Russell tours Gov. Pawlenty along with DECC board members and Mortenson staff.

The pessimists predicted failure. The optimists made their case for a sense of community pride and a vision for a brighter future. The result would not only determine the future of the DECC and downtown Duluth, but it would symbolize a broader perspective, for better or worse, on how Duluthians felt about their city's future.

On February 28, 2006, the community overwhelmingly responded by voting 61% to support the new arena. The vote revealed Duluthians' confidence that our community was worthy of an award-winning arena and didn't need to make do with good-enough facilities any longer. Our citizens rallied in support of a healthy downtown, strengthening our ability to compete as a destination, and more importantly, strengthening UMD's presence downtown and our university/community relationship as a whole.

It took three years of lobbying in St. Paul to finally get funding. The arena appropriation, which Gov. Pawlenty excluded in his 2006 bonding proposal, was also excluded in the final 2006 bonding bill. The state did not pass bonding legislation in 2007, failing to submit

Mary Sullivan

Construction complete — DECC employee and construction worker night prior to guest arrival.

a final bill by the end-of-session deadline.

Sen. Yvonne Prettner Solon, Rep. Mary Murphy, UMD Vice Chancellor Greg Fox, and City of Duluth Lobbyist Kevin Walli fiercely advocated for the project's success. Judge Gerald Heaney and Jeno Paulucci were heavily involved behind the scenes. (Jeno, questioning the governor's support, began jokingly referring to him as "Gov. Polenta.") But the governor was true to his word, and $38 million in state funding passed in the 2008 bonding bill. (It should be noted that the Minnesota Twins and Vikings ultimately received taxpayer funding for their respective stadiums, but without a vote.)

Mortenson Construction was hired and entered in to a guaranteed-maximum-price contract with the DECC Board. Cost overruns were not an option. Work began on what would become AMSOIL Arena.

As it turned out, the delayed funding may have been a blessing. By the time work began on the arena, Minnesota (and the rest of our country) was in the midst of the worst construction slowdown in a generation. For example, the tower crane used in constructing the

Brett Groehler

View from the catwalk, opening night game, UMD vs. North Dakota.

parking ramp attached to the new arena was the only one operating in the entire state at the time. (In the summer of 2015, there were five tower cranes operating in Duluth alone.) Thanks to 2008 legislation allowing the DECC Board to use a best-value approach to selecting contractors (instead of the traditional low-bid system), the project provided construction jobs for our local trades.

Nearly every contractor hired to work on the arena was from Minnesota, the vast majority from Duluth. The only exceptions were Superior Glass from across the bay (hardly an exception, really) and the only remaining U.S. arena seat manufacturer, Irvin Seating, from Michigan. Several local contractors have told me the arena project kept their businesses going and allowed them to retain their best employees through the economic downturn. Over 350 local union trade workers — our neighbors — built AMSOIL Arena.

One of the reasons Mortenson Construction was selected was their emphasis on safety. The Minnesota Department of Administration awarded AMSOIL Arena the MN Safe Award, the only project in outstate Minnesota to receive this award acknowledging a safe construction site. In the 400,000 trade hours needed to complete the new arena, not one day was lost due to a work-related injury.

Also, because of the construction climate, bidding was extremely competitive. For example, pile estimates in August 2008 were over $50 per foot. When we opened bids four months later, the low bid was less than $25 per foot. Multiplied by the 70,000 feet of piles supporting the arena, you get a picture of the savings that later went toward enhancing the facility.

The arena's design team was led by Brian Morse from Stanius Johnson Architects, Jim Swords from Populous, and Ron Kirk, the DECC owners representative.

There were several driving factors in the AMSOIL Arena design:

- Energy efficiency, with a goal to use 50% less energy than a typical arena;
  We met our energy efficiency goal, and the Arena received the LEED (Leadership in Energy and Environmental Design) Silver Recommendation.

- Not just meeting ADA (Americans with Disability Act) requirements but truly addressing the needs of our guests of all abilities;
  The number of spaces designated for guests with limited abilities far exceeds the ADA's requirement and are the best seats in the house.

- Incorporating local materials;
  Taconite became countertops. Reclaimed wood from Lake Superior became benches. Wood and terracotta blocks from the oldest grain elevator in Wisconsin, which was being torn down in Superior, became various design elements.

- And embracing the 1% For the Arts set-aside, reserving 1% of total construction cost to fund a public art element;
  The Duluth Arts Commission selected two artists, the late Joan Henrik and Teresa Cox, who designed and implemented, respectively, the Arena's spectacular award-winning terrazzo floors.

The DECC had one more opportunity: naming rights. The facility needed a way to differentiate the new arena from the original DECC Arena. DECC Board President Mark Emmel was an invaluable partner in creating the new arena, from funding through completion. Emmel arranged an informal lunch meeting with the late Al Amatuzio and other executives from AMSOIL to discuss naming rights. Two weeks later, an agreement for $6 million was signed. The new building had a name: AMSOIL Arena.

AMSOIL Arena opened on Friday, December 30, 2010. A good portion of the Duluth community showed up to AMSOIL Arena's grand opening celebration accompanying a UMD Bulldogs hockey game against the North Dakota Sioux. Over 7,000 fans watched Gov.-Elect Mark Dayton and Mayor Don Ness drop the first puck. Three months later, the UMD men's hockey team won their first national championship, beating Michigan 3-2 in overtime. The following evening, New Year's Eve, the Duluth Superior Symphony Orchestra dazzled a sold out crowd, presenting "Cirque on Ice" on the new arena floor. During the following few months, Michael Buble, Jeff Dunham, and Elton John performed. Rave reviews rolled in for Duluth's AMSOIL Arena. And in 2013, *Stadium Journey Magazine* rated AMSOIL Arena the best stadium experience for fans in North America. AMSOIL Arena, a world-class venue, came to be by the community's strong support and confidence — confidence, in turn, justified and reinforced by the arena's success. ∎

Dan Russell served as the Duluth Entertainment Convention Center's executive director from 1990 until he retired from the position in 2017.

AUTHOR ACKNOWLEDGMENTS

DECC staff was involved in every phase of the planning and construction of AMSOIL Arena.

Special thanks to:

Bob Hom	Joe Tarnowski	Steve Rankila
Chelly Townsend	Deb Aleff	Mary Sullivan
Caty Kaups	Sue Ellen Moore	Steve Rudh
Jeff Stark	Annette Eberhart	Wade Abrahamson

27

Duluth Transportation Center

BUILDING DTA'S MULTIMODAL HUB DOWNTOWN

by Jim Heilig

The Duluth Transit Authority (DTA)

is Duluth's main public transportation provider. And as longtime DTA passengers will remember, it's undergone quite an evolution to arrive at today's effective system centered in a modern multimodal transit station in downtown Duluth.

Today DTA bus service runs throughout the city and across the bridge to Superior, but Duluth's public transit system began in 1883 as mule-drawn streetcars on tracks spanning 11 blocks across downtown Duluth. Transit was focused on the downtown, where the jobs were.

The rail system expanded, added cable lines and electric power, and climbed the steep hillside. Stories of the railcars running up and down the vertical avenues still circulate in the community. The system evolved, ownership changed,

Duluth mule trolley on Superior Street circa 1896.

Superior Street station for the Incline Railway. This was the first main transfer station.

it merged with the Superior Traction Company, and in time, the DTA emerged as Duluth's primary transit system.

The City of Duluth acquired the DTA in 1969. At that time the DTA service was still focused on the downtown. As ridership continued to grow, the DTA faced many challenges in adapting to the increasing demand. In the early '80s, as part of the city's major streetscape project, the DTA added two new stops downtown to facilitate transfers and accommodate the pulse system, buses cycling through downtown every 15 minutes. With the addition of these stops, called super-stops or transit centers, passenger and auto congestion in these areas increased steadily.

GROWTH USHERS IN THE NEED FOR A NEW COMMAND CENTER

The most significant challenge of the present day has been the transit center on Superior Street between 2nd and 3rd Avenues West, which produced an array of issues on downtown Duluth's main thoroughfare and became a point of contention for nearby business owners.

In light of increased ridership and logistical challenges, the downtown business community has developed mixed feelings about the DTA system. Though the buses provide a reliable source of transportation for the flow of workers, shoppers, and tourists, business owners complained of buses taking up precious parking spaces, bus shelters blocking street views of facades, and increased traffic congestion. From within the center, it wasn't possible to see approaching busses, so crowds of passengers spilled onto the sidewalk to wait, clogging narrow sidewalks and hindering passers-by.

Bus-staging posed yet another challenge for the DTA. There was no place downtown for buses to wait inconspicuously in order to maintain their schedules. With limited options, the DTA sent buses to the M&H gas station 6 blocks away from the transit center to stage, a costly and inefficient setup.

The DTA reassembled routes in the early 2000s to decrease the number of needed transfers and hopefully alleviate the congestion and subsequent problems at the transit centers. Although the new routes, starting in western Duluth and ending in eastern Duluth without a transfer, served a subset of passengers well — western-dwelling hospital workers and UMD students, mostly — the new assembly wasn't working for all passengers, particularly mall area passengers. DTA convened with partners — Metropolitan Interstate Council (MIC), City of Duluth, Greater Downtown Council (GDC), and of course, its passengers — to study system improvements.

A set of short-term and long-term recommendations came out of these studies. In the short term, DTA should implement on-street modifications to improve the function of the downtown transit centers. And in the long term, DTA should pursue an off-street transit center.

The 2002 report read:

> **Long Term Improvements - Off-Street Terminal -** *A dramatic change to DTA operations would be the construction of an off-street terminal to accommodate DTA buses and boarding and alighting passengers. Operationally, DTA services would be focused at this downtown terminal. It could even be expanded into an intermodal terminal where transportation services other than DTA would be focused and could include long haul bus services, taxicabs and even rail passenger services. In fact, the terminal could even be part of a parking ramp for automobiles. There would be a number of benefits associated with an off-street terminal including:*
> *As DTA General Manager Dennis Jensen noted:*
> *"For years, the DTA struggled on where to place a downtown transit terminal that would provide a safe, accessible connecting point for its passengers. I've thought about this for 30 years."*
>
> **Resulting Benefits of a New Terminal:**
> *- Lowered operational costs*
> *- Improved access and security for riders*
> *- Provided transfer point for other forms of transportation*
>   *(including a possible high speed rail line)*
> *- Alleviated downtown traffic congestion with off street staging*
>   *of DTA buses*

- Improved relationships with downtown business owners
- Developed downtown connectivity
- Connections to major Bicycle Trails (per MIC Bikeway Plan)

Duluth will be a main stop for the Northern Lights Express (NLX), a proposed high-speed rail line. The NLX is three years ahead in its planning and development compared to most other high-speed rail lines in Minnesota. A new transit center could align well with the NLX vision.

The transportation center would also house related businesses, such as automobile and alternate transportation rental, courier, and tourism services. In concert with existing and future private developments, the center would serve as a connector to other downtown destinations and tourist attractions and the skywalk system.

There were a number of challenges related to an off-street transportation center. Finding a suitable site in the central downtown area stood out as the most prominent challenge. But other challenges included:

- Added running time to each DTA route in order to access the terminal;
- Increased walking distance for transit center users entering and leaving the terminal;
- Bus riders possibly opting to use other Superior Street stops (to avoid said increased walking distance), resulting in congestion at other stops;
- Building skywalk system access into the new facility;
- Steeply graded terrain in the central downtown area creates accessibility concerns.

And of course, an off-street terminal is a costly capital project. Downtown terminals in other cities have cost $10 million dollars or more.

LOCAL, STATE, AND FEDERAL SUPPORT

The DTA made short-term improvements while long-term planning began. Strong local, state, and federal support would be necessary to fulfill the long-term plan. The DTA contacted the late Congressman Jim Oberstar, who graciously engaged in discussions

Duluth Transportation Center on Michigan Street opened in 2016.

over the next several years to help establish funding for the project. The congressman worked to craft multiple federal programs, which served as potential funding sources for the DTA's project.

In 2006, a number of local efforts converged: the DTA was looking to move its downtown hub; the City of Duluth completed its comprehensive plan, which would bring about changes to its zoning codes; and the regional rail authority initiated efforts to restore passenger rail service connecting Duluth to the Twin Cities. To help

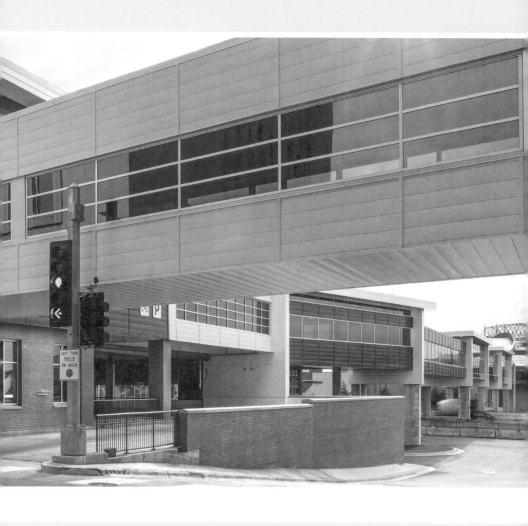

bring all these interests and stakeholders together, the GDC formed the Special Projects Task Force.

The task force identified primary transportation nodes and evaluated transportation methods and routes. The task force's studies and findings influenced the Duluth-Superior MIC's "Modal Connections Study," which assessed land use and transportation infrastructure between downtown Duluth, Canal Park, the Depot, the Duluth Entertainment Convention Center (DECC), and Bayfront Festival Park.

Inside the Duluth Transportation Center.

Of the task force's priorities, the most important items became:

1. Downtown Duluth multimodal transportation terminal for the DTA
2. St. Louis County's Duluth Union Depot (Depot) improvements for passenger rail service
3. Duluth multimodal connectivity projects for the City of Duluth (many of which completed by the DTA as part of its short-term plans).

The first two items were combined into a cohesive multimodal transportation initiative, and the DTA and St. Louis County jointly applied for a Tiger grant, part of the 2010 stimulus program.

St. Louis County's component involved redeveloping the Depot into a terminal for the NLX. Adaptive reuse of the Depot, which is on the National Register of Historic Places, would, in part, restore its originally intended use. The objective: facilitate intercity passenger rail service between the Twin Ports and Twin Cities while maximizing the development benefits of this service for Duluth and the St. Louis County region. The estimated cost: $85 million.

The DTA's component included ambitious construction of a new, off-street multimodal transit center, large parking ramp, and a three-block skywalk expansion, including a total rebuild of the portion of skywalk known as the Northwest Passage, which bridges I-35 to connect downtown and the DECC. The objective: alleviate downtown congestion and enhance citywide connectivity by building a central multimodal hub. The estimated cost: $63.8 million. The combined project totaled almost $150 million.

This project was ultimately rejected federally — the request exceeded funds available within the transit funding programs, and the NLX was not yet programmed for construction. The application was essentially deemed excessive and premature. A setback, indeed, but one which yielded a bountiful upside; besides producing a fleshed out project proposal and strengthening partnerships, the effort also attracted interest from local citizens and groups.

PROJECT RE-THINK AND STATE LEADERSHIP CHANGE

In a continued effort to direct funding toward this multimodal transportation initiative, Congressman Oberstar suggested the DTA separate its project from the county's project and additionally lessen its scope.

Thus in 2008, the DTA used a federal transit grant to further study needs and develop a new transit center concept. The study assessed potential locations, produced traffic concepts, considered connectivity, and drafted cost estimates. A stakeholders group organized around the task of recommending a site and concepts to the DTA Board. The board would then work to submit an application for federal stimulus funds and 2010 Federal Transportation Bill dollars.

The stakeholders group consisted of, in addition to the DTA, representatives from:
- City of Duluth
- St. Louis County
- St. Louis and Lake County Regional Rail Authority
- Duluth- Superior Metropolitan Interstate Commission (MIC)
- Downtown Building Owners and Managers Association (BOMA)
- Duluth Local Initiatives Support Corporation (LISC)
- Medical community
- Arrowhead Regional Development Council (ARDC)
- Minnesota Department of Transportation (MNDOT)
- Duluth Entertainment Convention Center (DECC)
- Greater Downtown Council (GDC)
- Canal Park Business Association (CPBA)
- Transit users
- Duluth Planning Commission

Congressman Oberstar advocated and crafted grant programs suitable for the project, and he assigned Bill Richard of his Washington staff to work with the DTA. All the while, city administration stood solidly behind the DTA.

The DTA put together a grant proposal for about $40 million in 2009. Just as grant review was about to begin, Congressman Oberstar and the Federal Transit Administration director suggested the DTA convert its grant to apply under a different program called the State of Good Repair. The State of Good Repair program was known to grant most selected projects half their request, and upon resubmission the following cycle, grant the second half. The DTA quickly turned around last-minute changes, submitted the grant as advised, and ultimately received $16 million, about half of its funding request.

Then in the fall of 2010 the transportation world changed as Congressman Oberstar narrowly lost the election. The newly elected congressman did not the support the DTA's project or other transportation projects across the state.

A NEW DIRECTION

The sea change prompted local groups and city administration led by Mayor Ness to rally with DTA and create an $8-million state bonding proposal. The city committed to uphold the DTA project as its top request for bonding dollars. Kristi Stokes at the GDC and David Ross at the local Chamber of Commerce endorsed and advocated for the project, and multiple other partners supported the effort locally and at the State Capitol.

The project's complexity, namely the element of renovating the Northwest Passage, gave state leadership pause. (The city owned the Northwest Passage skywalk with easement for the span over the freeway, and the DTA would administer the renovation work.) As the proposal worked its way through the Legislature, dollars available reduced as other projects gained quicker approval. The local delegation gave a final lobbying push near the end of the legislative session, and the multimodal center project won $6 million in state bonding money.

Thus, the DTA established a new budget of about $28.5 million for construction. The community and local agencies, especially the city and its staff, still had much work to do. As the DTA went into final planning and bidding on a design-build project, many of our partners joined us. The DTA set up committees that would assist in final design and then construction review. The DECC was a close partner, and Dan Russell and Chelly Townsend's leadership proved to be invaluable assets during the Northwest Passage discussions and construction. Cindy Voigt, the city engineer, worked diligently to coordinate multiple construction-necessitated road closures, including Michigan Street, Third Avenue West, the frontage road, and even the freeway. Cindy's expertise was critical in navigating these sensitive, essential closures upon which the project's success depended. Many project details required Planning Commission and City Council input and approvals along the way, and they, too, became key project partners.

The Duluth Transportation Center (DTC) opened in February of 2016 after 14 years of collaborative planning, seeking funding, advocating and rallying. By the center's completion, it had required multiple layers of approval, including from the federal transportation and labor departments; the state's transportation and natural resources departments, and the Historic Preservation Office; and local Planning Commission, City Council, and many more from the DTA Board of Directors.

Altogether, more than 25 groups and agencies supported and gave input over the course of the project. Congressman Oberstar got the project off the ground and the DTA's local partners, especially the city, led by Mayor Ness, fueled the progress, winning state funding and staying the course to completion. It was truly a community-driven project from start to finish.

The DTC provides an efficient, modern connection hub for passengers of various means, supports opportunities for future growth, and (especially within the broader transportation context) bolsters Duluth's role as a regional center. ∎

Jim Heilig began his career with the DTA in 1979 and recently retired from his position as the director of planning and adiminstration.

CHAPTER

28

NorShor Theatre

BRINGING PEOPLE TOGETHER AGAIN
AFTER 135 YEARS

by Christine Gradl Seitz

The grand doors of the NorShor Theatre, Duluth's historic downtown art deco theatre, opened wide on February 1, 2018, revealing a community icon of art and culture. That night represented the culmination of a remarkable community accomplishment defined by vision, grit, determination, and collaboration. We walked a long journey to reach that ribbon-cutting ceremony.

Today's NorShor Theatre has a long, winding history. It began in 1883 as Duluth's Grand Opera House. In 1940 it opened as the NorShor Theatre, an art deco film house. In 1982, the building was purchased by Erik and Deborah Ringsred, and took various forms as a music venue, independent movie theater, and creative gathering spot.

By 2010, the NorShor had fallen into disrepair and was a blight on a part of downtown that was in its very earliest stages of recovery. The theater's grand marquee promoted

(Above) The Orpheum Theater (1910-1939).

(Right) Built in 1940, NorShor's tower marquee stood 65 feet above the theater, weighed over 300 tons, and was removed in 1967.

the strip club operating inside. Duluth's most prominent historic theater had become a prominent embarrassment for the community and a burden on nearby businesses.

Historic theaters all across the country were being torn down because of neglect. The Palace Theater in Superior was torn down in 2006 and many believed the same would eventually happen to the NorShor unless a full restoration was undertaken.

If the NorShor was to avoid the fate of the Palace Theater, action was required. Mayor Don Ness developed a vision and plan for public ownership and restoration. Ringsred and Ness met to structure an agreement that would ultimately result in the full historic restoration of the theater. But the sale of the building was only the first step of what was to be a challenging journey.

The Duluth Economic Development Authority (DEDA) purchased the property in 2010. The most direct path to restoration would have involved public-debt financing ultimately paid with taxpayer dollars. But the choice was made to protect the taxpayers' interests by pursuing a more difficult, complicated, and challenging finance plan combining historic tax credits, state bonding support, new market tax credits, developer financing, and private fundraising. A team approach was needed.

The Duluth Playhouse — a nonprofit organization with more than a century of experience — had outgrown its venue at the Depot and needed to expand. The Playhouse became a key player in the Norshor renovation, creating a vision, purpose, and sustainability plan. An outside independent consultant was hired to conduct a feasibility study and create a proforma of what operations should look like for the NorShor to be a sustainable venue. It was determined that the Norshor would rely heavily on an anchor tenant — the Playhouse — because of the group's large patron base and support. But to be successful and sustainable, it would also require the usage of other arts groups, community events, and private parties.

The period from 2010 to 2014 held a great deal of study, research, and planning for NorShor's viability. The big question: what will the financial structure look like? When it was apparent that the costs of restoring this venue would be $20-30 million, we all knew that was not a price tag that could be fundraised in our community.

Enter Sherman Associates, an award-winning firm specializing in design, construction, and financing commercial and housing properties. They brought expertise in historic restoration projects and crucial experience securing new market and historic tax credits, state grants, and bonding.

A partnership was in place to make the restoration possible. DEDA purchased the building with plans to connect it to the skywalk. The city contributed Tax Increment Financing (TIF). The State of Minnesota provided $7 million in bonding, and Duluth LISC provided $750,000 for a pre-development loan. Sherman Associates garnered financial support through an array of resources including historic tax credits and new market tax credits. The Playhouse, as a nonprofit organization, would conduct a capital campaign and raise $4.5M for the project.

DEDA, the Playhouse, and Sherman Associates — along with the expertise of local architects TKDA and Johnson Wilson Constructors, and DRL Group, a Cleveland-based architecture firm specializing in historic theater restoration — took the paper plan into reality in only 18 months. The lightning speed deadline was a stipulation of the tax credits.

Our partnership brought a variety of experience to the restoration. The Playhouse brought more than a century of producing live theater and its knowledge of how a theater works. Sherman Associates understood construction with years of success restoring old buildings and community projects. The City of Duluth brought its support with a strong vision, operating plan, and due diligence to make sure the community was getting their beloved theater back.

Throughout construction, there were challenges, compromises, and concessions. Although construction plans were in place on paper, everything could change as soon as we started knocking into walls. As construction continued, different challenges crept up that we had to understand together and collectively come up with plan b. The team worked together beautifully.

One of the biggest challenges was the stage. Because it was most recently a movie house, there was no existing stage, and the stage space was limited. The back wall butts up against Second Avenue East, and the stage is boxed in between the temple and the alley. We could not achieve the wing space we would have preferred, but we developed a viable space for performances.

We would have liked a tunnel underneath the stage for performers to cross over, but we could not excavate any deeper because of bedrock. (And you don't use dynamite in a historic building!)

We were just able to dig out enough space for an orchestra pit, which was quite a concern for a while.

A movie house has a flat floor; the audience looked up at the screen. So we needed to rake the floor so the seating could be tiered. We brought the stage out as far as we possibly could and created tiered seating. Because we moved the stage out, we had to rebuild the entire balcony. It was tiered for the visual of a movie screen, but on a stage, that visual sightline drops. We raked the balcony deeper so everyone could see the stage.

Another interesting challenge was the matter of creating a scenic shop for building sets. NorShor sits on a steep hill: its front door opens to Superior Street, its back door opens to First Street's alleyway, and the actual stage drops a full 16 feet from the alley. The solution? We constructed a scenic shop on the second floor of the

Historic renovation efforts sought to both maintain and restore the classic historic features of the NorShor while providing modern amenities and stadium seating, ensuring all 605 seats have an excellent view of the stage.

Photos by
Dennis O'Hara/Northern
Images Photography

building. Sets are rolled out from the shop directly to the alley. They are then rolled down the alley to the stage door, where we built a lift to lower the sets onto the stage.

Some of the structural challenges inspired some exciting solutions. We achieved one of the most unique features of a venue like this: an interior lounge. Along with the mezzanine lounge, we have two lounge spaces available for pre-show, post-show, and private parties. These lounges have changed the theater-going experience for people; rather than arriving ten minutes before curtain, getting a ticket and their seat, patrons are arriving much earlier and enjoying a drink or something to eat in the lounges, which feel almost like a private jazz club. The lounges have created an intimate socializing space, which elevates the entire theater-going experience. Outside groups can also reserve these lounges for meetings and events. They provide an intriguing alternative to a standard ballroom.

The experience for Playhouse patrons turned out beautifully. Our attenders have been amazed at the seats, sound, and viewing. Over and over we hear that it's spectacular and beyond expectations to come in and sit and see everything so clearly in such an intimate space.

It shouldn't be surprising that the NorShor Theatre was able to bring together so many partners in a joined effort to restore and recreate an icon of the Duluth arts experience. That's what theater does – it brings people together. Theater, by nature, is a reflection of humanity: who we are, what's important to us, how we resolve conflict, and how we problem-solve. This project brought together a community of people who may not have otherwise been engaged. Ultimately, it is a reflection of our community. The restored NorShor Theatre became a reality because of our community's support of the arts and our belief in its importance to our quality of life. ∎

Christine Gradl Seitz is the executive and atistic director of the Duluth Playhouse, and now NorShor Theatre. With a background in professional theatre from Broadway to theatres across the country, Christine leads the way for the new vision of the restored NorShor Theatre that will promote local, regional, and national groups to bring new and exciting experiences to the community.

OUTDOOR SPACES

"The nation behaves well if it treats the natural resources as assets which it must turn over to the next generation increased, and not impaired in value."

—Theodore Roosevelt

CHAPTER

29

Bayfront Festival Park

LOIS AND JENO'S BAYFRONT LEGACY

by Gary Doty

During my twelve years as Mayor of Duluth, I enjoyed dozens of relationships that inspired the development of projects that helped make Duluth a great place to live, work, and visit. My relationship with Lois and Jeno Paulucci rises to the top of that list.

Those who knew Jeno in the business world were well aware of his gruff exterior. Believe me, as mayor I saw it more than once; and when Jeno had something he wanted done, he was never shy about letting me know. There were days when my staff would bring in volumes of faxes from Jeno, complete with his signature that filled nearly half a page; and I knew it was time to give him a call.

I was once told that the definition of an optimist is "someone who goes to work for Jeno Paulucci and brings his lunch." That was the Jeno that lived in local popular culture, but I was fortunate to see a side of Jeno that not

Aerial view of Bayfront Festival Park (from the west) and its surroundings.

everyone saw.

I experienced a kind man — an exceedingly generous man who wanted to give back, even as he built a business empire that rivaled any we've seen in this part of the world. In business, Jeno could be ruthless. But when it came to his hometown, there were very few things Jeno Paulucci would not do.

When I look at today's Bayfront Festival Park and the Lois M. Paulucci Music Pavilion, I am reminded that Jeno and his wife Lois changed our city for the better and did so with a grace and humility that spoke well of both of them.

In the late '90s, I received complaints about the condition of the bayfront area and the need to make it something greater for the community. Yes, the old tent was still up, the venue was attracting some good acts, and it served the community as the site for its annual Fourth of July celebration and fireworks display. However, Duluth is nothing if not a community where every passionate citizen has a different idea of how to make things better, and the bayfront area was no exception. Voices were calling for change.

At the time, I convened a task force charged with addressing the need for change and the differing opinions as to how we could improve the bayfront area. Some wanted to bring the retired USS *Des Moines* to the waterfront. Some wanted a shopping mall. Some wanted a movie theater. These are just a few of the dozens of ideas generated.

The one thing everyone could agree on was that a portion of the land needed to be saved for public use. That's where Lois Paulucci came in.

In all my conversations with Jeno, Jeno always said that Lois was the "boss." He meant it lovingly because he absolutely adored her. Consequently, it was one day in 1999 that I saw a side of Lois and Jeno which was, frankly, endearing. On that day, I contacted Jeno and asked that he consider building a recreation center somewhere on the waterfront. Jeno said he'd consider it, and within 24 hours responded saying, "Lois wants to create a first-class park on the bayfront." While the current venue was good, Lois thought it could be much better; and she was right. The old property didn't drain well and because it does rain in a Duluth spring, summer, and fall, the grounds were rarely in prime condition. Some major acts couldn't be booked at the site because they would have had to bring their own stages. When Bob Dylan and Paul Simon played at the bayfront, that's exactly what they did.

> "What you feel, standing there on that gentle knoll, is that you're glad to live in a city that pulled this off."
>
> —Sam Cook,
> *Duluth News Tribune*

Experience a Bayfront show from the land or water — boaters anchor in the harbor to enjoy the summer concerts. Ships entering the harbor make for a spectacular backdrop for those on land.

Lois was ready to help change all that. In September 1999, she agreed to pledge $2 million to help build what is now the Bayfront Festival Park. That spurred not only good ideas, but consensus. We, as Duluthians, wanted a festival park that could be enjoyed by all.

I asked a local promoter who had booked activities at the site in previous years exactly what his definition was of a "festival park." He replied, "It's whatever you want it to be." Right then and there I knew we had a blank slate on which to draw our plan.

Randy Wagner was the lead architect, and the pavilion he designed became the centerpiece for the whole project. That centerpiece and the area around it became the Bayfront Festival Park and the first-class venue it is today.

Soon we found that even the generous gift of $2 million Lois had pledged wasn't enough to complete the project. Lois quickly responded, "Then I'll add another million." — thus covering

75 percent of the eventual project cost out of her own pocket.

We knew we should do something special to thank Lois and Jeno, and I suggested to Jeno that we name the new facility after the two of them. Jeno's unforgettable reply was a bit of a surprise. With a smile that told me he was speaking tongue-in-cheek, he said, "All my life, I've built a reputation for being an s-o-b. I'm not going to ruin it now by putting my name on the park. It should be Lois' name."

The night of July 26, 2001, was indeed Lois' night. Fifteen thousand people greeted Lois and Jeno as they arrived in their car for the grand opening — Lois and their driver in the front seat and Jeno in the back seat — as they traveled to the backstage area. The *Duluth News Tribune* report of the evening recounts how I had promised Lois, who opposed the city's restaurant smoking ban largely because of the potential negative affect it might have on her son Mick's business interests in Canal Park, that she could smoke in my office if the bayfront plan came together. As I approached their vehicle, Lois promptly rolled down her window and playfully blew a puff of cigarette smoke in my face. It was a lighthearted and fun moment and one that I shared when I eventually had the honor of eulogizing Lois at her funeral.

The grand opening was a marvelous night — and not the first one at the new Bayfront Festival Park which involved the Pauluccis. Lois also wanted to see a skating facility at the park. On January 1, 2003, she pledged an additional $350,000 over and above her original gifts to help build the current Bayfront Warming House. Ground was broken in September, and the warming house opened the following year.

Now, when you look at the Railroad Street area and the development that's there, you can see that long after their initial gifts, Lois and Jeno are still impacting development in Duluth. I'm not convinced we would have seen development such as the Pier B project were it not for a revitalized Bayfront Festival Park.

The Bayfront Festival Park is used year-round — from Bentleyville, Minnesota's best winter holiday lighting show, to the Blues Fest in August.

There's an ambience at Bayfront Festival Park now that I believe is unmatched by any outdoor amphitheater in the country. It is stunning. Comedian Steve Martin once held up the start of his act for ten minutes so he and his fans could watch from the Bayfront Festival Park a thousand-footer pass under the iconic Aerial Lift Bridge.

What gives me special satisfaction when I look at the Bayfront Festival Park is best expressed in the words of the *Duluth News Tribune's* writer Sam Cook. He wrote, "What you feel, standing there on that gentle knoll, is that you're glad to live in a city that pulled this off."

Amen to that, Sam. None of it would have been possible were it not for the generosity of Lois and Jeno Paulucci. The next time any of us spend a perfect Duluth day at the pavilion which bears Lois' name, may we remember the legacy of Lois and Jeno Paulucci. ∎

Gary Doty served in the Minnesota House of Representatives (1974-76), the St. Louis County Board (1976-1991), and as mayor of Duluth (1992-2004). A Duluth native, Doty taught in the Duluth Public Schools, and with his wife, Marcia, owned numerous successful businesses including restaurants, an athletic camp, a laundromat, real estate developments, and health care for vulnerable adults. Doty's relationship with Jeno dates back to Doty's childhood days as a neighbor to the Paulucci family.

CHAPTER

30

Duluth Rowing Club

WELCOMING ALL ROWERS INTO THE 21ST CENTURY

by Tom Rauschenfels

Originally chartered as the Duluth Boat Club in 1886, the multi-faceted waterfront activity club's first building was located at the foot of Fifth Avenue West and the waterfront, basically where the present-day Great Lakes Aquarium stands. After departing that site in 1903, mainly because of increasing commercial vessel traffic and the associated problems with trying to maneuver long, narrow, fairly unseaworthy rowing shells on the busy waterfront, the Duluth Boat Club built a new boathouse/clubhouse on Park Point.

The new building was located at 10th Street South and Minnesota Avenue, between today's Lakehead Boat Basin and the U.S. Coast Guard station. The Duluth Boat Club's site eventually housed dormitories for rowers, a 75-foot

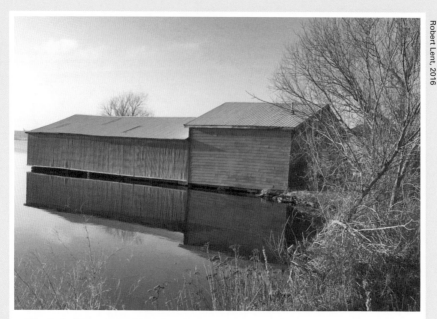

Robert Lent, 2016

The Duluth Rowing Club's old boathouse located at 3911 Minnesota Avenue, part of the Oatka Beach branch of the original Duluth Rowing Club, established in 1886. This boathouse was finally removed in January, 2017.

heated swimming pool, tennis courts, and storage for rowing shells, sailboats, canoes, and powerboats. Additionally, local philanthropist and boat club supporter Julius Barnes sought to establish branch clubhouses and boathouses at Oatka Beach (39th and Minnesota Avenue), Spirit Lake (up the St. Louis River), and Pike Lake (near the present-day AAA Auto Club site). This was the time of Duluth's most famous early-year rowers: Dave Horak, Doug Moore, Max Rheinberger, and Phil Moore, also known as the "Invincible Four" in 1916; and Walter Hoover, who won the Diamond Sculls Championship at the Royal Henley Regatta in Henley, England in 1922.

Today, all that remains of the original Duluth Boat Club's glory days is the Oatka Beach site. The Depression of the 1930s brought about the demise of the original Duluth Boat Club. It wasn't until 1955 that a group of former rowers, led by Max Rheinberger, resurrected the original Oatka Beach site, courtesy of the Park Point

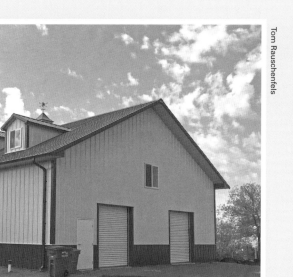

Tom Rauschenfels

Finished Duluth Rowing Club's 44x56' Clubhouse that contains locker rooms, showers, bathrooms, and storage for 28 double and single rowing shells. Completed in the spring of 2018, with landscaping to follow.

American Legion Post, which purchased the property. In 1978, the Duluth Boat Club was officially renamed the Duluth Rowing Club (DRC) to better show its strict focus on the sport of rowing.

Many harsh, icy winters followed by summer's high water levels ravaged the DRC's Oatka Beach boathouse. It had been a mission of the DRC's board of directors and executive officers to set aside a portion of each year's budget surplus, should there be any, to the possibility of building a new boathouse at that site. That is, until 2011, when the club got a wonderful surprise.

A longtime rower, club member and supporter, Joseph "Joe" M. Krmpotich, in his passing, left an unexpected gift for the DRC. Joe's love for rowing began when he was a young man in the late '60s through the early '70s when there was a resurgence of rowing in Duluth. Joe and his younger brother, Dave Krmpotich, rowed with the club. (An interesting aside: until that point, competitive rowing had been largely limited to men, but it was during this resurgence

Tom Rauschenfels

View of the finished, 63x63' Joseph M. Krmpotich Boathouse, looking east while standing on the ice of the Superior Front Channel, 3911 Minnesota Avenue. This building houses all the DRC's large rowing shells, including the 60-foot crewed eights, 40-plus-foot quads and fours, doubles and singles, along with oars and rigging components.

we saw the early days of women competing as well.) Dave went on to become a member of the 1988 U.S. Olympic rowing team from Duluth that won silver in Seoul, South Korea. It was upon Joe's passing in 2011 we learned of his undying support of rowing and the club's work to bring the sport to the community. He left his entire estate (roughly $400,000) to the DRC with the directive that it be used in the building of a new boathouse.

The DRC Board and club members formed a committee in light of Joe's legacy direction to explore permitting, design, and construction of a new boathouse. At that time, a steep learning curve guided the process. The first hurdle was learning which agencies controlled the permitting of waterfront projects.

Since the original Oatka Boathouse was built over the water, a rebuild required permission from the Minnesota Department of Natural Resources (DNR). As for the portion of the structure on land, the DRC discussed potential variances and permit restrictions with the City of Duluth. The eventual hiring of a waterfront engineering firm made much of the somewhat complicated process easier to understand and thereby made the final decision-making easier. Since the proposed new boathouse mimicked the original, the DNR ultimately decided it could be built over the water again, but with some restrictions. A new building could not exceed the original's square footage (40 ft. by 100 ft.; 4,000 sq. ft.) and could be no higher than the original at its highest peak (26 ft.). A particularly difficult restriction on the new facility: no plumbing. The original building included plumbing, but this time around, it wouldn't be allowed.

Project limitations eventually prompted the committee to return to some basic questions: what did the DRC want to achieve with a new facility, and did the current plan lend itself to that end? The DRC saw tremendous value in building a new home base to support the club's current activity and its drive to introduce one and all to the benefits of rowing. The home base would ideally include both a new boathouse and a clubhouse offering a health and fitness center geared specifically toward the sport of rowing. Solely replicating the existing boathouse wouldn't accomplish this goal. So the committee broadened the vision into the proposed Duluth Rowing Center, a modern facility with full accommodations to house a program for learning to row, and recreational, competitive, juniors (ages 13 - 19), open (19 - 27), and masters (27+) rowing. A clubhouse like this, alongside a new boathouse for storing equipment, would support the DRC's operation and growth. Thus began the pursuit of a new vision and fundraising campaign. Longtime rower, Jenny Peterson, agreed to lead the campaign, which combined with Joe's legacy, set the fundraising goal at $1 million.

The result is the second building phase: a 56-by-44-foot clubhouse, built entirely on land with the blessing of the City of Duluth.

The clubhouse is completely accessible (ADA compliant), and contains full plumbing and electricity necessary for running the program envisioned for the Duluth Rowing Center. The clubhouse includes locker rooms, showers, bathrooms, and a classroom. While the ultimate financial goal has yet to be reached, both buildings are loan-free, and as of this writing, money raised is at 96 percent of the finish line tally. In addition, the DRC plans to complete the final phase of the Duluth Rowing Center, including landscaping and floating, rowing-shell-friendly docks.

The Joseph M. Krmpotich Boathouse was officially opened and dedicated at the Duluth International Regatta on July 16, 2016. The DRC was fortunate to have Joe's brother, Olympic rowing silver medalist, Dave Krmpotich, both compete and be the featured speaker at the dedication.

There couldn't be a better time for the DRC to be healthy, growing, and ready for the next hundred years of rowing. From an environmental perspective, the community has invested dearly in the cleanup and ongoing stewardship of our coveted waters, Superior Bay, the St. Louis River estuary, and Lake Superior. Couple that effort with Duluth's commitment to protecting and expanding its outdoor adventure opportunities, citizens and visitors are increasingly drawn to explore the city's natural environment and waterways. Today's energy fuels a love and curiosity for outdoor recreation experiences in Duluth, and the DRC proudly welcomes everyone to discover and enjoy the silent, healthy, full-body-and-mind workout of rowing. ∎

Tom Rauschenfels grew up and has lived on Park Point near the Duluth Rowing Club for most of his life. Tom is a retired public school art teacher and has long participated in and advocated for silent water sports, including sailboat racing and cruising, rowing for recreation and competition, and kayaking.

AUTHOR ACKNOWLEDGMENTS

Last, but not least, the following individuals have been instrumental in the growth and success of the Duluth Rowing Club:

Greg Peterson, chief designer, planner, and organizer of the DRC expansion plans

Jenny Peterson, chairperson of "Continuing the Tradition" fundraising campaign

Michael Cochran, DRC historian and author of "Invincible, History of the Duluth Boat Club"

Arvid Brekke, integral in planning and design, as well as craftsman for both new buildings

Bonnie Fuller-Kask, head coach and director of rowing programs

CHAPTER

31

Trails and Outdoor Recreation

LEADING THE PACK

by Hansi Johnson

When I was a kid, my track coach pulled me aside at practice one day to address my ill behavior. He said, "Hansi, you can let the world define you, or you can define yourself."

My coach's words came back to me in 1989 when I first moved to Duluth — a city seemingly letting the world define it, afflicted with tired old stereotypes, unable to simply be itself. Duluth locals know those stereotypes well: too cold; too old; a failed industrial town with no jobs; a place of urban decay, depopulating faster than any other city in Minnesota; ecologically scarred; blah, blah, blah.

I wound up leaving Duluth for other work opportunities. But then I got a job as a sales rep for the Patagonia Clothing Company, and I could live anywhere in a five-state region of the Midwest. To me, it was a no-brainer. I wanted to live where I could be outside and embody my employer's brand, which aligned (then and now) with my personal values. The brand centered on (and still does) a life of adventure, being outdoors, being healthy, and promoting conservation. Duluth fit those themes perfectly (and still does).

But when on the road — regionally, nationally, and even, internationally — I was continually struck by how people reacted when I told them I lived in Duluth, Minnesota. Those old stereotypes kept popping up. Meanwhile, the Duluth I knew was a totally different place, a totally different experience than the stereotypes portrayed. And I knew that a large number of people were living in Duluth for the same reasons I was, and we didn't even think about the stereotypes. In fact, many of them were points of pride and celebration. Too cold? Not if you like to ski!

As my career in the outdoor industry progressed, I went from selling stuff to advocating for the very things I loved about living in Duluth. It was apparent to me that Duluth, as a place, had not yet realized its potential as an outdoor town. If we could cultivate what Duluthians already knew and loved about this place to change Duluth's identity, its brand, people would be more apt to visit, live, and work here.

We recognized early on what has now become a better-known trend: younger people are choosing where to live based on how the place matches the lifestyle they pursue, and they're figuring out the job issue later. They are picking place over position. This theme has been relevant to my generation, the Gen Xers, and even more relevant to the Millennials. Having easy access to world-class outdoor recreation tends to be high on young people's list when choosing a place to live and raise their families.

So take that concept, that lens, and place it over Duluth.

First, look at Duluth's location. Built on the shores of the greatest lake in the world — Lake Superior — and around the lake's largest watershed on the U.S. side — the St. Louis River — Duluth naturally has a lot of relief in its terrain. Duluth is a city of hills and water — something not typical to most Midwestern towns — and the sports you can do here reflect that. From an outdoor adventure and recreation standpoint, Duluth has been blessed by geography and geology. Its terrain perfectly suits hiking, trail running, skiing (downhill, XC), and mountain biking (downhill, XC), to name a few. And its water access adds paddling (flat-water and whitewater), sea kayaking, surfing, kitesurfing, fishing, sailing, rowing, power boating; the list goes on.

In Duluth, undeveloped open space sits right next to urban areas — a perfect juxtaposition for fast, convenient access to the natural environment. Within Duluth's city limits, there are 15,700 acres of undeveloped green space and 92 miles of water frontage.

At one point in the early 1900s, Duluth was growing so quickly it looked like it might outpace Chicago as a metro area. To meet that potential, officials at the time set its city limits 27 miles long (east to west) and five miles wide. That growth, of course, did not come to pass, and the result is a city with a dense urban core and vast open space on its east and west sides.

From the outdoor recreation perspective, this is a boon. It provides limitless opportunity to interlink trails of all kinds across the urban areas of the city. For locals, this means access to healthy trail-based activities just steps out their doors. And for outdoor recreation tourists, it means multi-day trail experiences without leaving the city.

Duluth's natural endowments make a marvelous place for the "outdoorsy" among us. And even if not "outdoorsy," Duluthians tend to share a strong appreciation for nature and its integral role in our

> I hear less and less of the tired, old stereotypes that the rest of the world used to paint on us. Now, people ask, "When's the best time to visit Duluth?"

Spread: Bouldering is amazing in Duluth's rocky terrain.

Inset left: Duluth's terrain is perfect for off-road cycling, for both scenic views as well as great riding.

Inset right: Duluth is a place shaped by water, and because of that, it's the perfect playground for paddlers.

Photos by Hansi Johnson

cityscape. And where people and place marry well, excellent programs are often born. The universities in the city, for instance, have long had great outdoor recreation programs, which have helped spawn a wealth of enthusiasts. The city also boasts some great outdoor clubs; groups like the Cyclists of Gitchee Gumee Shores (COGGS), the Duluth Climbers Coalition, the Duluth Cross Country Ski Club, the Superior Hiking Trail Association, and the Northland Paddlers Association are good examples of these organizations.

But it wasn't until city government broadened its role in supporting outdoor recreation that a sea change in perception took place. Historically, the city had not intentionally capitalized on Duluth's "outdoor town" quality until Mayor Don Ness became interested. His initiative to invest in and promote Duluth's natural assets garnered widespread attention.

Focus and collective energy began to build a framework for redefining Duluth. And soon it was time for a case study to see if public/private partnership could pull off next-level projects to make Duluth a premier outdoor adventure destination.

COGGS initiated the Duluth Traverse (DT) concept: a single-track mountain-bike trail that threads its way across the city from east to west, connecting five of Duluth's major parks and open spaces. The DT is a beginner-level off-road cycling trail that will be roughly 50 miles in length once completed. It intersects five other mountain-bike trail systems, thus creating a 100-mile interlinked trail system in the city

The creation of this mountain-bike trail system uncovered a host of challenges and opportunities. For instance, the DT started a healthy discussion about what land was important to the community and why. Preserving natural space requires proper ownership and reclamation of public lands. Intentionally holding certain corridors of access could allow the city to invest in activities that would pay dividends both in the health of locals and the dollars spent by visitors. The vast majority of Duluth's 15,700 acres of open space are not owned by the City of Duluth; they are tax-forfeited land owned by St. Louis County, and thereby unprotected. The city's commitment to long-term investment in natural assets necessitated, first, land access and possible acquisition.

The DT exemplified how a local not-for-profit group (COGGS) could leverage its membership and relationship with international partners, like the International Mountain Bicycle Association (IMBA), to design a world-class system and then raise the labor force and funding to create it. The city realized it had a partner with horsepower to help build an attraction that was both good for the community and for tourists. Thus, a model emerged in the relationship between COGGS and the City of Duluth — one that could be recreated with other user groups and their respective activities.

The case study helped contextualize outdoor recreation, and has broadened our collective understanding of its benefits to our community. Duluth, like any other city of its size, grapples with social issues. For example, locals are familiar with the east-west divide, rooted in some tangible factors: an aging population and subsequent stagnating housing stock in Duluth's western neighborhoods; a health disparity between the east and west sides of Duluth, evident by a shorter life expectancy amongst folks living in the west side. Couple these realities with the fact that the western half of Duluth houses the lion's share of the city's undeveloped open space, and it begged the question: could out-your-door access to world-class trails tempt new Duluthians to buy up stagnant housing stock on the west side as well as promote access to healthy living for those citizens who already lived there?

We knew outdoor recreation was by no means the only, or most important, factor to effect change in the western neighborhoods. But it proved to be a simple tool that paid tribute, in a sense, to the extraordinary, collective river cleanup efforts that took place over the previous several decades. The St. Louis River Area of Concern restoration work spoke to our community's environmental stewardship and resolve; it set a foundation on which to build the next layer of investment.

The Mayor pulled the Minnesota Land Trust (and myself) into the conversation in 2014 to consult on a vision centered on Duluth's west side and its potential to use its open space to attract new workers,

Hansi Johnson

Very few cities have both urban amenities and world-class recreation layered on top of each other, but Duluth has just that, across the entire city.

retain existing workers, and rebrand Duluth as an outdoor town.

We started the process by asking the outdoor user groups — those who used outdoor spaces now and would have the greatest insight on improvements — to tell us what destination-quality experiences would look like here. In these conversations, I challenged the user groups to brainstorm projects that embraced Duluth's attributes, versus trying to become something we are not.

These working groups brainstormed projects, and many gained traction:

- Extend the Duluth Traverse across the west side from Observation Hill to Chambers Grove Park.

- The Duluth Cross Country Ski Club (DXC) proposed a new, cutting-edge Nordic Center with snowmaking at the base of Spirit Mountain Recreation Area.

- The Duluth Climbers Coalition (DCC) proposed a new city park in the abandoned Duluth Sand and Gravel Quarry to include, unlike any other city park in the country, an ice-climbing facility.

- The Duluth paddling community proposed a National Water Trail along the St. Louis River Estuary. This designation, given by the Rivers, Trails Conservation Assistance program (a division of the National Park Service) is non-regulatory but gives the river a new identity — one that promotes getting people back on the water after the amazing amount of work that has gone into its restoration.

- The local walking and hiking community proposed destination hiking loops off of the famous Superior Hiking Trail (SHT). The loops, staggered along the 45 miles of SHT running through the city, would provide more options for short, quick walks and hikes.

The mayor then tasked the city's Parks and Recreation Department with starting a rigorous public process to gather input from neighborhood groups, stakeholders and other regulatory agencies, and land managers who could partner to develop these projects.

The public process was thorough, arduous and successful. Projects became more inclusive and mainstream for all types of users. The resulting suite of projects was named the St. Louis River Corridor Initiative, which the mayor and his staff presented to the City Council to receive a unanimous vote of approval. Advocacy for the initiative at the State Legislature paid off with an $18-million bonding measure awarded to its projects. And each user group accepted a dollar-for-dollar fund-raising challenge to match bonding dollars received toward their respective projects.

Bonding legislation moved the projects from concept stage to the more granular master planning stage. Four years in, the projects are at various stages of development. Each one has undergone a master planning and design process.

- The Duluth Traverse is the furthest along — about 85 percent complete — and it has prompted IMBA to bestow its highest recognition on Duluth, the IMBA Gold Level Ride Center designation. Duluth is one of only six Gold Level Ride Centers in the World. COGGS membership has risen from 50 to 650 people. The group has raised hundreds of thousands of dollars for the Duluth Traverse and gives back over 4,000 volunteer hours to the community annually.

- The DXC is in the early stages of completing the Grand Avenue Nordic Center. DXC has raised more funds, more quickly than any other organization in the city, raising nearly $500,000 in less than a year.

- In the early stages of the public process, the DCC went door to door to meet the neighborhood folks. It helped raise the funds to purchase the quarry property from the private firm that owned half of it. DCC has since put on two winter fund-raising festivals in the quarry, garnering high attendance, surprisingly by non-climbers and climbers alike. DCC volunteers have built a new ADA accessible trail to access the quarry floor and a new Frisbee golf course.

- The master plan for the National Water Trail is complete, detailed, and robust. Having the master plan completed allowed stakeholders to apply for the National Water Trail designation. This application has passed the nomination committee with flying colors and now awaits the final signature for designation by the current secretary of the interior.

• Several day-hikes, which will spur off of the Superior Hiking Trail, are in the works. Destination-worthy trails in their own right, the day-hikes allow folks access to the nationally recognized SHT without having to walk out and back each time.

Even though the river corridor projects are midstream, Duluth has received national attention for the investments its made in recreation. Just in the last two years, Duluth has received over 20 national print stories on the effort, uncountable web and social media stories, and numerous local and regional TV and radio stories. The Outdoor Writers of America Association held its 2017 national conference in Duluth. That conference brought nearly 400 writers to our community to learn more about our work and vision for Duluth's future.

Most importantly, the perception of Duluth has changed radically. Duluth has finally shed the world's characterizations and begun to define itself. Locals take pride in our city and landscape more than ever. While traveling, I hear less and less of the tired, old stereotypes that the rest of the world used to paint on us. Now, people ask, "When's the best time to visit Duluth?" ∎

Hansi Johnson has been an advocate for the positive power of outdoor recreation for most of his life and has lived in Duluth on and off since 1989. Johnson currently works as the director of recreational lands for the Minnesota Land Trust. Johnson is also a proud husband of Margaret Harstad and a proud father of his son Tae.

AUTHOR ACKNOWLEDGMENTS

Massive change does not occur through the work of only one person. In the realm of working on re-framing Duluth as an outdoor community, I would like to thank the volunteers who have worked thousands of hours to make numerous projects reality.

And specifically, thanks to the following people for stepping up and motivating their organizations and their membership to get involved:

COGGS

Adam Sundberg
Waylon Munch
Pam Schmitt

DXC

Annalisa Peterson

Duluth Climbers Coalition

Dave Pagel
Lucas Kramer

Northland Paddlers Alliance

Scott Nuestal
Cindy Little

Duluth Sail and Power Squadron

Mary Brisky

Youth Outdoors Duluth

(an organization doing the truly hard work of connecting ALL kids in the city to Duluth's outdoor recreation)

Melody McKnight

City of Duluth Parks and Recreation

Jim Filby Williams
Jim Shoberg
Lisa Luokkala
Parks and Rec Staff

CHAPTER

32

Leif Erikson Rose Garden

A HISTORY RETOLD IN ROSES

by Mary A. Tennis

1968 LEIF ERIKSON ROSE GARDEN

Duluth's Leif Erikson Rose Garden has undergone several evolutions. The original rose garden was planted in 1930 under the direction of then-park-superintendent, F. Rodney Paine, and included 30 roses cared for by the Duluth Garden Flower Society. The garden's historical record between its 1930 origin and its first evolution in the late '60s is vague, if not nonexistent. The garden may have been abandoned at some point between these two incarnations.

The garden's first big evolution came in the late 1960s when Ausma (John) Klints wished to thank the Duluth community for the warm welcome she received upon immigrating to Duluth from Latvia. Ausma envisioned a 1,200-rose garden overlooking Lake Superior, inspired by examples she'd seen in Europe and Australia. She designed

1968 Rose Garden.

the garden as an expression of her gratitude. Virginia (Joseph) Sellwood and Sigrid (Wildey) Mitchell raised money to fund the realization of Ausma's vision. Out of this partnership, the Duluth Rose Society was established on September 6, 1967. The city's parks department employees prepared the garden for planting in 1967, and the Rose Society planted roses in the spring of 1968.

Klints' garden design showcased a granite horse fountain, which had been donated to the city by Clara Blood in 1905 in honor of her father, George C. Stone, Duluth's first treasurer. The fountain originally stood at the intersection of London Road and Superior Street where it watered horses. In the late 1920s the fountain was moved to Lake Shore Park (renamed Leif Erikson Park in 1929) where it remained unused until 1968. The city couldn't afford to repair the rusted pipes at that time, so William Sweeney, a member of the Duluth Rose Society, stepped up to design a plumbing system for the fountain and an irrigation system for the garden, and the local Plumbers Union came forward to complete the work on the fountain. This volunteer effort restored the fountain for its next life at the center of the new garden.

The Rose Society's thoughtful care of the Rose Garden won it the honorable designation as a public display garden for All America Rose Selections, Inc. (AARS) in 1970. The society cared for the garden, with help from Duluth Parks Department, until 1985 when Parks took over management and care under the leadership of Helen Lind, city gardener at the time.

INTERSTATE 35 EXTENSION

An early proposal of the I-35 extension through downtown Duluth jeopardized the future of the Rose Garden. The plan required the garden's removal. A proposed freeway built on tall piers paralleling the waterfront would run through the garden's location, and effectively separate the community from Lake Superior, not only at the garden site, but along its entire track through downtown Duluth.

Coalitions formed in opposition of the proposal, citing major concerns, including access to Lake Superior, continuation of neighborhood cohesiveness, and preservation of historic buildings and the Rose Garden. In late 1975, Mayor Robert Beaudin appointed the I-35 Citizen's Advisory Panel, comprised of opponents and proponents of the initial freeway extension, and the panel partnered with the Minnesota Department of Transportation, the Federal Highway Administration, and the City of Duluth to create, and ultimately adopt, a revised I-35 extension plan.

The new plan came to be the design we know today. The project still required initial removal of the Rose Garden, but provided the opportunity to restore space and rebuild the garden. In 1989, roses were removed from the garden and sold to the public and the fountain was placed in storage in preparation for the freeway construction. I-35 was built to follow the waterfront through downtown Duluth and travel through a series of tunnels — tunnels topped with extensive landscaping designed to keep connections to the water intact. The Rose Garden was restored at its original location at 13th Avenue East and London Road, only this time, on top of a freeway tunnel, bridging the eastern part of downtown and the waterfront. The freeway design also led to the development of the community's treasured Lakewalk and was ultimately recognized nationally as one of the best designs in the interstate system.

The upper portion of Leif Erikson Park, which includes the Rose

A name is a name is a name

Today's Leif Erikson Park was originally referred to as Cullum Park, after Duluth Mayor Marcus Cullum. It was later called Lake Shore Park. Then in 1927, the replica of the *Leif Erikson* Viking ship sailed from Norway to the Duluth Harbor. Bert Enger purchased the replica ship and donated it to the city with the request it be installed at Lake Shore Park and the park be renamed Leif Erikson Park. The city officially renamed the park in 1929, and the replica ship resided there for many years. Eventually the ship was moved to storage to await the completion of a protective structure. Plans are in place to re-establish the boat in Leif Erikson Park in the future. ∎

Garden, and the Lakewalk were designed by Kent Worley, a local Duluth landscape architect. The city's gardener, Helen Lind, helped with garden design and chose the roses to plant. The new Rose Garden was patterned after an English formal garden and incorporated design ideas from the original 1968 garden. Its creation is a shining example of successfully integrating community involvement and the urban planning process.

1994 LEIF ERIKSON ROSE GARDEN

1994 marked another major evolution of the Rose Garden. The freeway tunnel beneath the Rose Garden had created an interesting microclimate with colder winter soils slowing spring rose growth. Reconstruction of the Rose Garden began in the spring of 1994 and included recreating the soil base; installing a retaining wall, extending the eastern side of the park by a half-acre and broadening the unobstructed vista of Lake Superior; addition of a stairway at the western entrance to connect the upper and lower portions of Leif Erikson Park and link the Rose Garden to the Lakwalk; and reinstalling the horse fountain as a garden centerpiece, restored to full function with a dog watering hole at its base.

About 2,500 new rose bushes were planted that spring, adorning

Tom Kasper

The Leif Erikson in the Duluth Ship Canal, 1927.

People from all walks share the pathway through the Rose Garden's lush offerings, season after season.

what had become the new Leif Erikson Rose Garden. The garden was once again chosen to become an AARS public display garden in 1997, and it displayed AARS roses until the organization disbanded in 2013.

DULUTH PARK MAINTENANCE DIVISION

Since 1994 the City of Duluth has managed the Rose Garden and is primarily responsible for its maintenance. Tom Kasper, who became city gardener when Helen Lind retired in 1995, kept the Rose Garden a priority of the city's park maintenance division for the 17 years he served in that role. The division's supervisor, Dale Sellner, has continued to provide leadership in caring for the Rose Garden since 2012.

The Rose Garden's dynamic microclimate poses plenty of

Mary A. Tennis

challenges to the crews that care for it. For instance, a simple wind shift can drop the temperature 20 degrees within 15 minutes.

LAKE SUPERIOR ROSE SOCIETY AND COMMUNITY VOLUNTEERS

The Lake Superior Rose Society formed in 1996, and along with other volunteers from the community, provides assistance with Rose Garden upkeep. Wayne Jesswein, who had been a member of the earlier Duluth Rose Society, organized local rose-growers and served as the new Society's first president. The Society continues to build on its 21-year commitment to fostering and sharing rose-growing knowledge. Members have helped with annual summer pruning and other major projects in the Rose Garden every year since the

Tom Roi *(left)* and Carol Borich of the Lake Superior Rose Society volunteer in the rose gardens.

group's inception. The Society partners with Parks staff to stage the annual Rose Festival, which coincides with the Society Rose Show in July and offers demonstrations of rose care, garden tours, and Q&A opportunities. The Society has written grants for garden signage upgrades and regularly helps with special projects.

EVOLUTION OF THE
1994 LEIF ERIKSON ROSE GARDEN

The park has undergone many changes since its 1994 overhaul, including the addition of a new bench, and railings, a planter and obelisks by city welders. A memorial garden for Ausma Klints was installed on the west end of the park to honor her vision. In 2002, Duluth community member Elizabeth Donley partnered with the city to add a peony garden at the east end of the Rose Garden. Elizabeth designed the peony garden and continues to volunteer for its management and maintenance. A new rose display featuring old garden roses, hardy shrub roses and companion plants was also added in 2002, and the Duluth Superior Area Community Foundation funded its improvement in 2009.

Aside from physical changes, the rose-growing and care methods continuously evolve. A commitment to sustainability and emphasis on aesthetics drive this ever-budding process. Today's collection of roses includes numerous disease-resistant varieties, a new display of Canadian hardy roses, and several rose beds used for testing the resiliency and hardiness of roses new to the park and its unique microclimate.

The overall number of roses has not changed dramatically since the last big addition in 1994, but the garden's plant population is more diverse than ever. And the ratio of tender to hardy roses has shifted significantly. The original planting included mostly tender roses (hybrid tea, grandiflora, and floribunda). Now, gardens consist of more hardy roses and their companion plants. The garden contains more than 350 varieties of roses, and experimentation with different varieties and types is ongoing.

It requires dedicated attention and follow-through to keep the Rose Garden healthy and thriving. For instance, during the very cold Duluth winter of 1995/96, we tested several winterizing methods on the tender roses to determine best practices in our extreme winter climate. The Minnesota Tip Method proved superior to any of the other methods we tried. Even though a fair number of roses were lost that winter, we learned how to better fortify the gardens and maximize their odds of surviving Duluth winters. An impressive volunteer effort brings people to the Rose Garden every fall to tip roses, and community members donate bagged leaves used to cover and protect the rose plants through the winter.

PUBLIC APPRECIATION FOR
THE LEIF ERIKSON ROSE GARDEN

We know the Rose Garden is treasured within the community. When presenting a story about the Rose Garden, KBJR news anchor Michelle Lee referred to it as "our beloved Rose Garden." But visitors from around the world grace the garden's paths as well. An estimated 1.5 million people visit the Lakewalk each year, and the Rose Garden is a common Lakewalk stopping point.

The Rose Festival, weddings, band concerts, flower tours, brown bag lunches, dance performances, walkers, photographers, painters and dreamers are all a part of the garden's fabric. Community members' dedication to the Rose Garden — whether through membership to the Lake Superior Rose Society, work for city parks, or individual and group volunteer efforts — symbolizes a need to create and nurture beautiful spaces. It takes countless hands and partnerships to cultivate such an environment. The garden is alive; seasons cycle; the work is infinite. Perhaps in the human spirit, something blooms along with the roses. ∎

Mary A. Tennis retired from the City of Duluth after 24 years in its parks and recreation department and park maintenance division and served as the Rosarian for the Leif Erikson Rose Garden for 21 years. Mary currently serves as co-president to the Lake Superior Rose Society, of which she's been a member since its 1996 inception.

EPILOGUE

YES, WINNERS WE ARE

by Emily Larson

First seated at the desk of Mayor, one thing immediately grabbed my attention: an overwhelming, almost lonesome, sense of quiet. Sitting there for the first time — door shut, eyes wide open — after months of campaigning, anticipation, planning. All that talking, all those meetings, led to this: a long moment of silence, work waiting. I'd not yet realized how hard the job would get, how much could go wrong. Or how incredibly generous, resilient, tenacious or wonderful our Duluth community is.

The seclusion of that first startling moment didn't last long. Soon the phone rang, people knocked at the door, and I was off and running the mayor marathon.

Three years into the work, I've learned, time and again, that nothing worth doing gets accomplished alone. The number of people instrumental in the revitalization of the NorShor, for instance, could literally fill every seat in the theater.

But, as shown over and over through this collection, it takes that one bold vision to get each effort started.

I frequently refer to Duluth as the perfect incubator — small enough to get things done, big enough to matter. We take risks here, often because we can, but more often because we have to. *The Will and the Way* books (both volumes) are filled with risks that paid off.

And certainly, unwritten chapters abound with the risks that didn't — the "almost, but not quite" projects, also known as failures, that led to the big ideas and bold thinking we read about now.

We need both the successes and failures. The first is the balm, which heals the hurt of the second.

I'm asked often about what it's like to be the first female mayor of Duluth. I'm never quite sure how to answer that, since I don't know anything different. What I do know, however, is that my service is possible because of the very same determination, risk-taking, resilience and bold vision of generations of women before me: the successful council campaigns of Lucile Roemer, Meg Bye, Cynthia Albright, Yvonne Prettner Solon and all the women who came after.

By the time the next volume of *The Will and the Way* is published (and let's be honest, even though we are humbled Duluthians, we all know there will be more for us to be proud of), time will have passed. Another mayor will be writing this reflection. Hopefully more leadership barriers will be broken — in our city, in our state, in our nation.

My prediction: our grit, determination, focus — our ability to get big things started and over a finish line — these qualities will remain. It's who we are.

In the meantime, I'll do my part, if you do yours. Let's consider this page a bookmark, not an ending. After all, who am I to write an epilogue to a story that's still being written?

In appreciation,

~ Emily

Emily Larson was elected mayor of Duluth in 2015 with 72 percent of the vote. She is a parent, partner, trail runner, snowboarder and full-time admirer of Lake Superior.

INDEX

Photo captions are indicated in bold face type.
Publications are indicated in italic type.

I

J

M